1es

L 29 / PART 1

ıry–April 2013

Edited by **Lisa Cherrett**

Guidelines © BRF 2013

The Bible Reading Fellowship
15 The Chambers, Vineyard, Abingdon OX14 3FE
Tel: 01865 319700; Fax: 01865 319701
E-mail: enquiries@brf.org.uk; Website: www.brf.org.uk

ISBN 978 1 84101 760 0

Distributed in Australia by Mediacom Education Inc., PO Box 610, Unley, SA 5061.
Tel: 1800 811 311; Fax: 08 8297 8719;
E-mail: admin@mediacom.org.au
Available also from all good Christian bookshops in Australia.
For individual and group subscriptions in Australia:
Mrs Rosemary Morrall, PO Box W35, Wanniassa, ACT 2903.

Distributed in New Zealand by Scripture Union Wholesale, PO Box 760, Wellington
Tel: 04 385 0421; Fax: 04 384 3990; E-mail: suwholesale@clear.net.nz

Publications distributed to more than 60 countries

Acknowledgments

Printed in Singapore by Craft Print International Ltd

Suggestions for using *Guidelines*

Set aside a regular time and place, if possible, when you can read and pray undisturbed. Before you begin, take time to be still and, if you find it helpful, use the BRF prayer.

In *Guidelines*, the introductory section provides context for the passages or themes to be studied, while the units of comment can be used daily, weekly, or whatever best fits your timetable. You will need a Bible (more than one if you want to compare different translations) as Bible passages are not included. At the end of each week is a 'Guidelines' section, offering further thoughts about, or practical application of what you have been studying.

You may find it helpful to keep a journal to record your thoughts about your study, or to note items for prayer. Another way of using *Guidelines* is to meet with others to discuss the material, either regularly or occasionally.

Occasionally, you may read something in *Guidelines* that you find particularly challenging, even uncomfortable. This is inevitable in a series of notes which draws on a wide spectrum of contributors, and doesn't believe in ducking difficult issues. Indeed, we believe that *Guidelines* readers much prefer thought-provoking material to a bland diet that only confirms what they already think.

If you do disagree with a contributor, you may find it helpful to go through these three steps. First, think about why you feel uncomfortable. Perhaps this is an idea that is new to you, or you are not happy at the way something has been expressed. Or there may be something more substantial—you may feel that the writer is guilty of sweeping generalisation, factual error, theological or ethical misjudgment. Second, pray that God would use this disagreement to teach you more about his word and about yourself. Third, think about what you will do as a result of the disagreement. You might resolve to find out more about the issue, or write to the contributor or the editors of *Guidelines*. After all, we aim to be 'doers of the word', not just people who hold opinions about it.

Writers in this issue

Keith Beech-Grüneberg is Director of Local Ministry Training for the Diocese of Oxford, and Programme Director for the Local Ministry Programme at Ripon College Cuddesdon. He has a PhD in the Old Testament, and particularly enjoys teaching courses on preaching and on the Bible.

Henry Wansbrough OSB is a monk at Ampleforth Abbey in Yorkshire. He is Executive Secretary of the International Commission for Producing an English-Language Lectionary (ICPEL) for the Roman Catholic Church, and lectures frequently across the globe.

David Spriggs is a Baptist minister who has worked for the last 15 years with Bible Society, helping the churches and Higher Education to engage more fruitfully with the Bible. His passion is to see Christians enjoying their faith more and growing in their love for God and people.

Margot Hodson is Vicar of Haddenham Benefice in Buckinghamshire. She has taught Environmental Ethics at Oxford Brookes University and is on the boards of The John Ray Initiative and A Rocha UK. Margot's books include *Cherishing the Earth*, with her husband Martin (Monarch, 2008).

Janet Fletcher is Team Vicar in the Rectorial Benefice of Bangor. She offers spiritual direction and enjoys teaching groups in prayer, faith and spirituality, and leading quiet days. She has written *Pathway to God* (SPCK, 2006).

Robert Mackley read history and theology at Cambridge University before ordination. Fr Robert is currently Vicar of Little St Mary's, Cambridge. He is a published church historian and a regular columnist and reviewer for the *Church Times*.

Margaret Guite is an Anglican priest. During the 1980s she taught doctrine in two colleges of the Cambridge Theological Federation. Since then she has been serving in various parishes in the Diocese of Ely and is currently parish priest of St Mark's, Cambridge, and an honorary canon of Ely.

Patrick Whitworth is the Rector of All Saints, Weston Bath with North Stoke and Langridge. He served as Rural Dean of Bath from 2003 to 2008. He has published six books, including *Prepare for Exile* (SPCK, 2008), *The Word from the Throne* (2011) and *Paul as Pastor* (BRF, 2012).

David Fleming is a Baptist minister. After studying for the ministry in Oxford and specialising in Old Testament Theology, he has been minister of churches in Medway in Kent and Abingdon in Oxfordshire.

The Editor writes...

We start this issue on a high note, with a fortnight of studies on 'Blessing' (from Keith Beech-Grüneberg, a new contributor to *Guidelines*), followed by two weeks on Psalms 101—113, with an emphasis on praise, from regular writer Henry Wansbrough. The beginning of a new year is a good time to think with gratitude of our reliance on God and his faithfulness to us.

Our Gospel studies this year come from the second half of Luke, and David Spriggs begins our exploration with notes on chapters 14 to 17. This section has something of a party atmosphere, with its focus on communal meals and celebrations, and the joy of finding lost things. Yet there are conflicts not far from the surface, with the threat of worse to come, as Jesus looks toward Jerusalem for the last time.

In our world today, we are often reminded of threats on the horizon, and Margot Hodson tackles one of them from a biblical perspective in her notes on 'Environment'. She finishes, however, on the theme of hope and, throughout, brings a vision of a cosmos that was created to be good and continues to be loved by God.

We then move into more contemplative mood, as Janet Fletcher writes on Prayer in the New Testament and Robert Mackley (who brought us notes on Christmas two years ago) guides us through his reflections on Passiontide, leading up to Easter Day.

After Easter, we dive into Isaiah 19—39 with Maggie Guite, wrestling with some of the mysteries involved in God's dealings with ancient national and international politics. Then Patrick Whitworth shows us Paul's approach to pastoral leadership in 2 Timothy, Titus and Philemon. The issues addressed in these three short letters might also be described as political, albeit on a smaller scale than Isaiah's concerns. Whatever the arena, however, we are encouraged to endure hardship or apparent chaos, trusting in God's overarching control.

Finally, we spend two weeks looking at the story of Isaac, a somewhat neglected figure in Genesis. David Fleming offers some sympathetic insights into Isaac's character and spiritual growth, ending with an emphasis on blessing that brings us back full circle to the theme of our opening set of notes.

From the next issue, we welcome David Spriggs as Commissioning Editor of *Guidelines*, and look forward to meeting more new writers as well as some familiar names.

Lisa Cherrett, Managing Editor

The BRF Prayer

Almighty God,
you have taught us that your word is a lamp for our
feet and a light for our path. Help us, and all who
prayerfully read your word, to deepen our
fellowship with you and with each other through your love.
And in so doing may we come to know you more fully,
love you more truly, and follow more faithfully in
the steps of your son Jesus Christ, who lives and
reigns with you and the Holy Spirit,
one God for evermore. Amen.

Blessing

Blessing is something that Christians, and many other people, do a great deal. There are formal blessings in churches—for example, at the end of many services. There are quick 'bless you's when someone sneezes. And there are many more or less carefully thought-out blessings in speech, in emails (I have a colleague whose standard email signature is 'Blessings' before her name), in letters and on Christmas cards. We bless people, animals, food and much more, and we also talk about blessing God.

So what is blessing? Is it an expression of hope that good things will happen, or is it more than that: might a blessing actually cause things to happen? In either case, how could it be right for a human to bless God? Who can bless? How should we bless? The aim of the next fortnight is to look at different aspects of blessing in the Bible, to lay some foundations for considering questions such as these.

Blessing is a significant element of the Bible. Words translated 'bless' (at least in the New Revised Standard Version) occur over 400 times in the Old Testament and over 100 times in the New. These words fall into two groups. We will primarily be looking at passages using words from the Hebrew root *brk* (in the Old Testament) or the Greek *eulogeo* and related words (in the New Testament). These are the most common words and, as we will see, they are central to key biblical passages talking about both creation and redemption. They are also the words used to talk about people blessing, including the example of Jesus himself blessing the little children (Mark 10:16) and blessing his disciples as he parted from them (Luke 24:50). However, 'blessed' sometimes instead translates the Hebrew word *ashre* or the Greek *makarios*, and we will have an example of this when we look at the Beatitudes (Matthew 5:3–12).

Our studies will begin by looking at what happens in the Old Testament when God blesses and when people bless others, and what it means for people to bless God. In the second week we move from the Old Testament into the New Testament to see how blessing relates to Christ.

1 In the beginning, blessing

Genesis 1:1—2:4

In the account of creation with which the Bible begins, God pronounces three blessings. He blesses the birds and sea creatures (1:22), humankind (v. 28) and the seventh day (2:3).

The blessing for the birds and sea creatures is an instruction to them to be fertile and to fill the air and sea. Humans are similarly to fill the earth. A link between blessing and fertility is very common in the Old Testament. As a result, some scholars have argued that blessing was originally some kind of fertility force. However, this downplays the fact that, as here, blessing is closely linked to the activity of God, and is therefore not any kind of impersonal force.

Furthermore, the blessing on humans is not limited to fertility. More broadly, blessing brings prosperity to its recipients. In different blessings, different aspects of prosperity are highlighted, but prosperity often includes fertility, since, in the ancient world, having many children (or the multiplication of birds or animals) was seen as obviously a good thing, and probably the most important part of prosperity. In the contemporary Western world, it may not seem so vital: we have pensions to support us in old age, we are less directly dependent on agriculture and we are aware of the dangers of overpopulation. However, we still rely on the continuing vitality and fertility of the created order, of which we humans are part, and blessing is often about the natural processes working well, rather than anything working beyond them.

The blessing for human beings, as well as giving them fertility, offers them 'dominion' over the other living creatures (1:28). We are all too well aware of how this gift can be misused, inflicting lasting damage on the earth. It is important to note that, in Genesis 1, dominion is given to those who, in the previous verse, were created in God's image (v. 27). When humans act faithfully in accordance with this image (which most probably means acting as God's vice-regents on the earth), they will use their capacities well. Our ability to exercise a large measure of influence over our environment is a responsibility but also a great privilege, which offers many advantages for us.

The blessing on the seventh day is rather different. The benefit of this blessing is not for the day itself but for the rest of creation. After a period of work (God's work in creating, or human work in exercising dominion), there is a time for rest and recreation. This is a gift from God, as well as a necessity, which some of us find difficult to hold on to in the midst of our frenetic lifestyles.

2 The results of blessing

Deuteronomy 28:1–14

The book of Deuteronomy is set at the time when the people of Israel are on the verge of entering the promised land after their 40 years of wandering in the wilderness. The middle section of the book (chs. 6—26) gives the detailed laws that Israel is meant to follow in the land. These laws are preceded and followed by encouragements to the people to do as they have been commanded. Chapter 28 lists blessings that will follow if Israel is obedient, then curses that will come if they are disobedient. Similar lists of blessings and curses are found elsewhere in the Ancient Near East, including in international treaties: Deuteronomy presents the covenant between Israel and God as similar to a treaty in which a group of people acknowledge a more powerful king as their sovereign.

The picture is one of abundant prosperity. Blessing 'in the city' and 'in the field' (v. 3) means blessing everywhere, just as blessing 'when you come in' and 'when you go out' (v. 6) implies that the people will receive blessing whatever they do—in all their undertakings (v. 8). It will be experienced in the fertility of the people, their crops and their animals (vv. 4, 11). In verse 4, it is expressed as a blessing on the crops and animals themselves, but the parallel blessing on the 'basket' (presumably used to gather the produce) and 'kneading-bowl' in verse 5 makes clear that it is the benefit they give to the people that is in view.

Verse 7 adds a further element to the blessing—that of protection. Israel will be secure to enjoy the prosperity given to it by God. Protection is also implied in the promise that Israel will be God's holy people (v. 9): if other nations see and recognise this status, they will be careful how they treat Israel, since it is dangerous to interfere with the holy or what is God's (v. 10). However, being God's holy people does more than increase Israel's security. It is an immense privilege to be the recipient of God's care and to be aware that this is the case; and it is important to have a sense of identity, to know fundamentally who one is. The Old Testament vision of blessing and prosperity is inescapably material but not limited to the material realm.

3 A blessing in worship

Numbers 6:22–27

It is unclear how these verses are meant to fit at this point in the book of Numbers. They seem to have no particular connection to what comes before (laws relating to the 'nazirites') or to what follows (offerings made once the tabernacle had been consecrated). However, they clearly fit as a closing blessing in worship, since they are still used in this way in many Christian and Jewish traditions.

Aaron and his sons (that is, the priests) are to use these words when they bless their fellow Israelites (v. 22). However, as verse 27 makes plain, the words are effective only because, when the priests utter them, God himself blesses the people. The power lies not in the words themselves or in the priests, but in God's commitment to act in a certain way when the priests speak the words. We might compare this to the Eucharist: we expect to receive grace when we receive Communion because we trust in God's commitment to act in a certain way when we do certain things with faith. So the priests are not just asking God to bless, but declaring or invoking God's blessing. The people leave worship bearing the name of God ('put on' them by the priests, v. 27): they are blessed because they are his. Silver amulets from the seventh or sixth century BC, displaying the words of this blessing, show that some people chose literally to carry God's name as a symbol and reminder of the blessing.

The words of blessing consist of three parallel lines (vv. 24–26), with (in Hebrew) three words in the first line, five in the second and seven in the third. Each line consists of two halves, the first half invoking an attitude of God towards the people and the second half expanding on it. In verse 24, God's attitude is that of blessing, and the result is that the people are kept safe from anything that might harm them. In verse 25, God turns a friendly face to the people, treating them in accordance with his grace: to say that God will give them a beaming smile goes a bit beyond the text but conveys the idea quite well. In verse 26, God looks with favour on the people, with the result that he gives them *shalom*. This word is normally translated 'peace' but denotes all-round well-being, a good summary of what God's blessing brings.

4 Blessing that cannot be undone

Genesis 27:1–10, 18–19, 26–40

What a mess! Time and again the Bible shows us God's purposes being fulfilled despite the all-too-human motivation and action of the people involved. But what do we learn from this passage about blessing?

Probably the most striking thing about blessing in this passage is that it apparently cannot be undone. When Isaac discovers that he has blessed Jacob rather than Esau, he cannot withdraw the blessing. Jacob gets to keep it, despite his deceit. Some scholars have seen in this a kind of primitive, magical understanding of blessing. However, in Genesis 29 there is a very similar situation in which the tables are turned on Jacob: he thinks he is marrying Rachel, with whom he has fallen in love, but Rachel's father Laban substitutes her older sister Leah at the last minute. Jacob discovers the deception the next morning, but no one assumes that it invalidates the marriage. Similarly, nowadays, once someone has become a godparent they cannot lose this status (at least, not without renouncing Christian faith entirely). There is a way to become a godparent, but not a way to stop being one. In Genesis, there is a way to bless (and to marry), but not a way to withdraw blessing (or withdraw from marriage).

As we saw yesterday, according to Numbers 6:22–27, when the priests bless (that is, when they utter a blessing), God blesses (bestows prosperity). In Genesis 27, when Isaac utters a blessing, God bestows prosperity (vv. 28–29). God's blessing is invoked or declared rather than just requested. The setting here is in the home rather than the temple or other place of worship. However, it is a formal context—that of a father and (in Old Testament terms) head of the household at the end of his life (vv. 1–2), giving his blessing to his son. There are similar end-of-life blessings elsewhere in the Old Testament, although they are all given when death is imminent rather than as a precaution in case death should come (Isaac does not actually die until many years later: see 35:27–29).

In verses 39–40, Isaac does his best for Esau. Obviously it is not the kind of blessing that Esau would have chosen. His life will be away from the rich and fertile lands that Jacob will enjoy (compare verse 39 with verse 28), and he will be subservient to his brother. But he will live, and he will be able to break free. If blessing is an effective invocation of God's action, it must respect the reality of God's purposes for the person's life. It is not a place for expressing unrealistic hopes.

5 Blessing in everyday life

Ruth 2

We have already seen people blessing in formal contexts—priests in worship and a father with his sons. In this passage we have examples of people blessing each other in everyday life.

In verse 4, Boaz and the reapers working for him greet one another. Boaz invokes God's presence with them; in response they invoke God's blessing on him. Blessings were commonly given in ancient Israel when people met or parted (see, for example, Genesis 47:7–10). It is certainly possible that people sometimes used the words without thinking about their original meaning, just as, in English, the parting phrase 'God be with you' has lost its original force and become shortened to 'goodbye'. But Boaz seems very aware of God's role in human life and the importance of God's blessing (see v. 12, though the word 'bless' itself is not used), so it is unlikely that his greeting in verse 4 uses God's name in a casual or unthinking manner. He wants the reapers to know God's presence, and he would hardly welcome a casual or flippant response from the reapers, which fails to take God's blessing seriously. So their first thought, like his, is the importance of what God does: ultimately, the success of anything they and Boaz might do depends on God's blessing. Are we as conscious of God in our everyday interactions?

In verses 19–20, Naomi responds to Ruth's account of her day gleaning in the fields. She offers a blessing on the man who has helped Ruth, and repeats it when she learns that the man in question is Boaz, a member of their family. As a poor woman, recently returned from a foreign country, there is nothing she can offer him in return for his kindness, other than the most important thing of all. When someone helps us, are we as likely to bless them or pray for them as to thank them in some other way?

6 Blessing God

Psalm 145

What does it mean to bless God? In Hebrew, the word 'bless' is used four times in Psalm 145—in verses 1b, 2a, 10b and 21b. English translations vary. If you read the psalm in the New International Version, for example, you will not come across the word 'bless' at all, while the New Revised Standard Version uses 'bless' in all four verses.

We can get a good idea of what it means to 'bless' God by looking at the other halves of the verses in which the idea occurs, since, in Hebrew poetry, it is common for the first and second parts of each line to be closely related. The two halves of the line do not say exactly the same thing in different words, but they do frequently express two different aspects of the same thing. So blessing God is closely related to lifting him up or extolling him (v. 1a), praising his name (v. 2b), giving him thanks (v. 10a) and speaking his praise (v. 21a). Blessing God is neither more nor less than responding to his goodness with thanks and praise. The rest of the psalm, of course, gives many examples of why God is indeed worthy of that response. As the psalm expands on God's goodness, the 'I' who blesses God in verses 1 and 2 is joined by other faithful people in verse 10, until, in verse 21, all flesh is blessing God's holy name.

What has this got to do with blessing other people? The most likely explanation is that people sometimes said, 'May you be blessed' to a fellow human as a way of thanking them or praising them. What better response is there to someone's good qualities than asking God to bless them (see, for example, Ruth 3:10)? What better return can we make for a favour than asking God to bless the giver (see, for example, 1 Samuel

23:21)? Of course, some people still say 'bless you' today when they are grateful for something. The word was used so commonly by people who were thankful to or admiring of another person that it also became used when people were thankful to or admiring of God.

We should note that although we may 'bless' God because he has 'blessed' us, when we say that, we are using the word in two very different ways: his blessing increases our prosperity, but our actions cannot increase his.

Guidelines

We have seen this week the importance of God's blessing—of God's granting prosperity to people (in particular). It includes concern for the material dimensions of life: blessing isn't something that exists on a separate plane from food and money and security, although it is not limited to these things. We have seen, too, that God gives humans the privilege of invoking his blessing. Priests and farm workers, men and women, young and old can all do this, and can expect that God will act in response to their words. Do we make use of this incredible privilege?

Of course, though, we have to ask the question: do things actually work like this? It is not obvious that the people who have blessings invoked on them in the world today actually prosper more than those who do not, just as it is far from obvious that those who trust God and are obedient to him do better than those who ignore God. Faithfully attending worship and being blessed at the end of it—whether now or in centuries past at the temple in Israel—is not an infallible route to obvious success.

The Old Testament writers are well aware that things do not always work as they 'should' (for example, see the book of Job or Psalm 73) and they are prepared to let confident affirmations of faith stand alongside acknowledgment of the complexities. In the case of prayer, many Christians maintain their belief that praying for someone or something does make a difference (did not Jesus promise that he would do what we ask in his name?) without a naïve assumption that, every time they pray, they can be certain that what they ask for will happen. Should we likewise confidently affirm the importance of blessing, at the same time as wrestling with the question of why there is not clearer evidence of it in the world around us?

1 Blessing for all nations

Genesis 12:1–3

At the start of last week, we saw how blessing is part of the fabric of creation. Today we begin to see that it is also part of God's plan of redemption.

After the account of creation in the first two chapters, Genesis 3 to 11 tells how humanity repeatedly goes wrong—in the garden of Eden (ch. 3), when Cain murders Abel (4:1–16), before the flood when all human thought is 'only evil continually' (6:5), and then at the tower of Babel (11:1–9). Each time, God acts to limit the consequences and undo some of the damage—except that the account of the tower of Babel ends with God scattering the people, and no sign of his grace (11:9). Only when, at the start of chapter 12, God speaks to Abram (later Abraham) does it become clear that he has not given up on humanity.

No reason is given for God's choice of Abram. There is no preparation for these words. God just speaks to him, telling him that he needs to leave his country and kin behind (v. 1), but promising him great reward (vv. 2–3). Abram's descendants will become a great (meaning 'numerous') nation, even though his wife Sarai is barren, making it unclear where his descendants will come from (11:30). Abram will be blessed: God will make him prosper, in part by having these descendants. Abraham's reputation will be great, as others will see that he is a signal example of God's blessing (if people are said to be 'a blessing' in the Old Testament, it means that they are notably in receipt of blessing, not that they are a source of blessing). God will protect him, since people will discover that if they favour him, God will bless them, while if they abuse him, God will curse them. And he will have the honour of bringing blessing to all the families of the earth.

Translators of the final part of verse 3 differ on whether they think the nations will 'be blessed', 'find blessing' or 'bless themselves' (that is, say 'may we be blessed as Abraham is blessed'). Some of the arguments are to do with Hebrew grammar and cannot be summarised here. However, in context it makes perfect sense that what God is starting with Abram should ultimately be his way of restoring his relationship with humanity in general—although it will take some time for that to happen.

2 Those who believe are blessed with Abraham

Galatians 3:6–17

How can Gentiles come into relationship with God and gain his blessing? Throughout the first chapters of Galatians, Paul is confronting that issue. Some Jewish Christians were trying to persuade the new Christians in Galatia that they needed to go beyond faith in Christ, becoming obedient also to the Old Testament law. Paul is adamant that Gentiles do not need to take this further step. Once they have put their trust in Christ, they have received the Holy Spirit and done all that they need to do. (It is important to note that Paul here is not contrasting faith with 'works' but with 'the works of the law'. The issue is not the place of 'doing things' in the Christian life, but specifically the place of the Old Testament law.)

Paul's argument takes us back to the Old Testament, and particularly to what Genesis says about Abraham, the ancestor of the Jewish people. Since it was Abraham's trust in God that was the foundation of his relationship with God (v. 6, quoting Genesis 15:6), Paul argues that when Gentiles share this attitude, they count as Abraham's spiritual descendants (v. 7). Subsequently, Paul makes explicit the point that God did not give his people the law until many years later (v. 17). So when God promises to Abraham that in him the whole world will be blessed (v. 8, picking up Genesis 12:3 and the related promises later in Genesis), it is through believing like Abraham—and not by obeying the law—that other people will come to share the same blessings that he received.

Of course, it is the coming of Christ that makes this blessing possible. The promise to Abraham was a prophetic announcement of the gospel, not something that could be experienced at the time it was made (v. 8). It is Christ's death that deals with the 'curse of the law' (v. 13). 'In Christ', Gentiles receive blessing (v. 14): Christ is the promised offspring of Abraham who will extend the blessing to Gentiles (v. 16) and the one in whom they put their trust (2:16).

Paul does not spend much time spelling out what the blessing means. The dispute in Galatia was about how to get it, not what it was. However, in verse 14 he does note one aspect of the blessing—that believers receive the Holy Spirit. The Holy Spirit works in believers to guide, transform and empower them (v. 5; 5:16–26); but the Spirit is also a promise, a kind of first instalment or guarantee of fuller life to come (2 Corinthians 1:22; 5:5; Ephesians 1:14). We shall be looking at this further in our next study.

3 Spiritual blessings

Ephesians 1:3–14

A standard form of Jewish prayer was and is still the *berakah* (the Hebrew word for blessing). Such prayers begin by praising God, and are introduced with 'Blessed be God' or 'Blessed are you, O God'. Here in Ephesians, the prayer is one long expression of praise. Indeed, in the original Greek, it is just one sentence, as the reasons for the praise keep spilling out without (as it were) there being time to stop and draw breath.

The reason why God is praised is summed up in verse 3: he has 'blessed us in Christ with every spiritual blessing in the heavenly places'. The following verses then give examples of those blessings. They begin before creation as God makes his plans for people to be restored to him in Christ (vv. 4–5, 11). God then redeems us by Christ's blood, forgiving our sins (v. 7). Thus he adopts us as his children through Christ (v. 5). In these ways he has poured out the riches of his grace upon us (vv. 7–8). He has also made known to us his will eventually to bring together all things in Christ (v. 10), giving us, in Christ, a share in that future (v. 11). Since we have trusted in Christ, we have received the Holy Spirit, in part to assure us of our inheritance to come (vv. 13–14).

From that summary it is clear how Christ is involved in every part of God's blessing activity towards us. 'The heavenly places' are where Christ is with God and where believers already are (1:20; 2:6). We must be careful, therefore, not to draw too sharp a distinction between what happens 'in the heavenly places' and the reality of our everyday existence: Christ will indeed bring together everything 'in heaven and... on earth' (v. 10). The same is true when we hear the word 'spiritual': the spiritual realm is not separate from the material world in which we live (as Western post-Enlightenment thought tends to assume) but is, in part, a dimension of that world. So 'spiritual blessings in the heavenly places' go beyond material blessings on the earth, since they link us to a greater reality, present and future (with the Holy Spirit in us connecting us to that reality). But they should not be sharply contrasted with material blessings on the earth. The New Testament does not suggest that God has lost interest in people's present material prosperity, but that the future and the non-material are more important.

4 A Christian blessing

Hebrews 13:20–25

Most of the letters in the New Testament end with a blessing. As here in verse 25, it is often God's grace that is invoked. The best-known example of this is taken from 2 Corinthians 13:13: 'The grace of our Lord Jesus Christ, the love of God, and the fellowship of the Holy Spirit be with you all.' When all else that is necessary has been said, the most important thing is that the recipients of the letter continue to enjoy God's unmerited favour and the gifts he freely gives.

In Hebrews 13, however, there is another blessing, in verses 20–21. We should note that in neither of these blessings is the word 'bless' actually used. There are no magic formulae for blessing, or particular words that have to be said. Whenever we invoke God's favour towards someone or his action in their life, we are blessing—whatever words we use and however many or few they are.

Verse 20 describes the God who is called on to bless. He is the 'God of peace', who establishes good relationships between himself and humans and within humanity. Since the Greek word *eirene* was commonly used to translate the Hebrew word *shalom* (see Hebrews 7:2), this peace goes beyond the absence of strife to denote the quality of relationship that allows people (and all creation) to flourish. This is now possible through Jesus' death and resurrection—his blood sealing the covenant that is everlasting, as God had always intended it to be.

Verse 21 describes the content of the blessing. It balances what God does in us with our living for him. He shapes us and our lives in good ways: we might say that he makes us people of peace, in the rich sense of the word 'peace' that we have just seen. The result of God's action in us is that we will be ready to fulfil his purposes. So in and through us he brings about what he wants, establishing that peace in the world. Is this true of our lives? And is it a vision that we share when we bless others?

5 The blessed life

Matthew 5:1–12

How can we tell whom God favours? The Beatitudes make very clear that whether a person seems to be prospering—whether the person is even happy now—is no firm guide. God's favour is on the poor in spirit (v. 3), those who mourn (v. 4) and those who are persecuted (vv. 10–11), none of which are states that most people would choose. Being meek (v. 5) or merciful (v. 7) or a peacemaker (v. 9), or hungering and thirsting for righteousness (v. 6), is less obviously contrary to present prosperity, but certainly does not always go along with it. (In Luke's version of the Beatitudes, 6:20–21, attention is focused even more on present material wants, since there Jesus says, 'Blessed are you who hunger now' and 'Blessed are you who are poor'—not 'poor in spirit'.) Present suffering is real and may be genuinely painful. Christians should never try to pretend otherwise or seek suffering when it can be avoided. But sometimes the attitudes that bring eternal reward (such as inheriting the earth, seeing God, or being called God's children) may lead, in the short term, to suffering. Then, that suffering is worth enduring.

The word translated 'blessed' here, in most versions of the Bible, is the Greek word *makarios*, which is not related to the word *eulogeo* used in the other passages that we have considered. Moreover, in the Old Testament there is a Hebrew word, *ashre* (see, for example, Psalm 1:1; Proverbs 28:14), which is not related to the word *brk* used in the passages we have been studying, but is translated as *makarios* in the Septuagint, the Greek translation of the Old Testament. *Makarios* (like *ashre*) is used to declare that someone is fortunate: it is not used to invoke God's activity. People said to be *makarios* are being congratulated by the person speaking, and held up as models, rather than being blessed by that person. 'Blessed' is probably still the best translation: 'happy', as we have seen, is quite possibly what the people are not; 'fortunate' makes it sound as though fate or chance, rather than God, is responsible. But it is not helpful that, in English, we have only one word where Greek and Hebrew have two.

If we wrote a set of Beatitudes, whom would we include?

6 Jesus took bread and blessed

Mark 6:30–44

If you looked at the title of today's study before you looked at the passage, you may have been surprised to find yourself reading the story of the feeding of the 5000 rather than the account of the last supper. Taking bread and blessing is indeed what Jesus did at the last supper (see Mark 14:22–25), but that was because it usually happened at normal Jewish meals. Just as Christians today might say grace, many Jews did, and do, thank God for their food by saying a prayer of thanks beginning 'Blessed are you, Lord God almighty…'. Whether at the last supper or when feeding the 5000, Jesus blesses God for the food rather than blessing the food itself. (Some translations say that Jesus 'blessed it/them' in verse 41, but there is no word for 'it' or 'them' in the Greek.) In Luke's account of the last supper, the word 'bless' is not used; instead, Jesus is said to give thanks (Luke 22:19; see also 1 Corinthians 11:24).

So, at the point when he blesses, Jesus is not doing anything special to the bread (or the fish): he is not imparting to it the power that will cause it to multiply, or making it particularly holy. Nearer to the truth is a comment in the Tosefta, a compilation of Jewish traditions, probably from around AD250: 'One who makes enjoyable use of the world without saying a blessing over it is guilty of profane use of sanctified matter.' Jesus is not making the bread good enough to eat or to be multiplied. Rather, he is acknowledging that it is already God's good creation and God's gift to humanity, before he makes the good use of it that God intended.

Do we think of the material world as something to be enjoyed with thankfulness because it is a way in which God blesses us?

Guidelines

The picture we have built up of blessing in the New Testament is a trinitarian one: God the Father blesses us in Christ through the Spirit. Most significant is the redemption won for us by Christ's death and resurrection, with its eternal consequences, of which the Holy Spirit gives us a foretaste now. But we should not conclude from this that blessing is only about redemption or that the consequences are only for the future. God's kingdom is already present, though we have to wait for its fullness. There are signs of that kingdom, even if we may wonder why there are not more. The Old Testament picture of blessing is not wrong, even if, in the light of Christ's coming, more needs to be said.

The New Testament gives us examples of Christians blessing others, as well as telling us that Jesus blessed children who were brought to him (Mark 10:16) and his disciples (Luke 24:50). The question for us, then, is not whether we should bless other people but how we should do so. When we put intercessory prayer into words, what we ask for is a mixture of what we know God always wants (for example, that people may trust his presence with them), what we tentatively believe we may be discerning about God's will in each particular case, and what we hope for. Perhaps we should bless in the same way.

At the end of these two weeks of studies, here are some final blessings for you to receive, whatever your particular circumstances:

'May the God of peace himself sanctify you entirely; and may your spirit and soul and body be kept sound and blameless at the coming of our Lord Jesus Christ. The one who calls you is faithful, and he will do this' (1 Thessalonians 5:23–24)

'Peace to all of you who are in Christ' (1 Peter 5:14).

'The Lord be with your spirit. Grace be with you' (2 Timothy 4:22).

FURTHER READING

Keith Grüneberg, *Blessing: Biblical Meaning and Pastoral Practice*, Grove, 2003.
James Jones, *People of the Blessing: God's love as found in the Psalms*, BRF, 1998.

Psalms 101 (100)—113 (112)

The psalms are Israel's prayers, and one prominent element in them is praise. Many of the psalms begin 'Hallel' or 'Alleluia', which means 'Praise the Lord; praise YHWH'. But what is praise, and what is the point of it? Another expression of it, in Mary's canticle, is 'My soul magnifies the Lord.' But how can I 'magnify' God? I cannot make God any greater, and nothing I can give will contribute anything to God.

Plato raised this point long ago in the *Euthyphro*, in his discussion of what piety is. If piety is 'service of the gods', how can I serve the gods or contribute anything to them? Am I to be like a child who, having received the ideal present, dances around showing it off and talking about it to all and sundry? Do we, in the same way, just want to talk about all we have received from the Lord, and by so doing praise the Lord? Of course this doesn't do anything for God, but it puts us in the right relationship to God just by expressing our thanks and our appreciation of the awesome majesty of God.

These notes are based on the Revised Grail Psalter and, unless otherwise stated, on the New Jerusalem Bible. *A note on numbering:* The Revised Grail Psalter, in accordance with the Roman Catholic tradition, uses the numbering of the Greek version of the Psalms, rather than the Hebrew. In the Greek text, the Hebrew Psalms 9 and 10 are shown as a single psalm—Psalm 9. Thus the Greek version stays one number behind until Psalm 148. Because many Protestant versions adopt the Hebrew numbering (following Luther's preference), however, both numbers have been given in psalm references between 10 and 147. You will find the Hebrew number given first, with the Greek in brackets afterwards.

14–20 January

1 I sing of love and justice

Psalm 101 (100)

This is a Wisdom psalm, reflecting on the qualities and way of life that are the aim of a life well ordered. It would be entirely mistaken to dismiss it as boastful or arrogant, proclaiming the singer's own achievements and qualities, although we must admit that the reticence and modesty demanded by our age have no place in biblical thought. So the apostle Paul can say, 'Be imitators of me, as I am of Christ' (1 Corinthians 11:1). Nor is it useful to describe the hymn simply as a series of good resolutions.

The psalm should be read and prayed as a reflection on the divine qualities described, and a plea for them. It is, after all, addressed to God. It begins with a reflection on two salient qualities of God's dealings with his creation. God's *hesed* (love) gives us hope in despair and failure. We need not rely on our own achievements, our own strength or abilities, our own righteousness. *Hesed* makes home and family a source of reliance and refuge, the quality that every child (young or less young) seeks in a mother and a brother or sister. There, if nowhere else, the failure and the sinner can expect a welcome and forgiveness. In our dire need, a mother's sternness and a sibling's rivalry fall away, to leave raw and open the welcome and sympathy needed by a failure. Moses experienced this forgiving love (in Exodus 34:6) when, after Israel's blatant idolatry, the Lord defined himself as full of tenderness and compassion, rich in *hesed*. Ever since then, we have relied on this as the defining quality of God.

The other quality hymned by the psalmist in the first line is 'judgment' (NJB). This means God's decisions or verdicts, as in a law court. Usually God's *hesed* is paired with *'emet* or 'truth, trustworthiness'. Here it is more about the decisions that emanate from this quality than the quality itself. Verse 2 twice uses the word that means 'complete, blameless'. Rather than wanting to escape from due blame, the psalmist is praying for a fulfilled life, for completion and satisfaction, that God's decision will go the right way. If we believe in divine guidance, there is no such thing as 'luck'. A prayer that God's decisions may be complete, and that the psalmist may live a fulfilled life, is the believer's equivalent to wishing for good luck.

2 Do not hide your face from me!

Psalm 102 (101)

The logic and thrust of this psalm are not immediately clear. The early and late parts of the psalm (vv. 1–11 and 24–28) seem to be the lament or complaint of someone who is grievously sick and slipping towards death, while the central part (vv. 12–23) is a hymn of praise to the Lord in expectation of the re-establishment of the primacy of Jerusalem after the exile. So distinct are these two parts that they are often thought to be separate compositions, clumsily combined.

The clue to the unity of the composition is in verses 2 and 28, which bracket the psalm. Each refers to 'your face', although in verse 28 this is often translated 'your presence'. In fact, the expression used is 'before your face'. In each, the issue is the confrontation of the psalmist with the Lord—a saving confrontation that brings assurance and serenity. This is the theme of the psalm, at the beginning a plea not to withdraw this presence, and at the end a peaceful repose in that presence. Amid all the horrors so vividly pictured in the early section (withering like cut grass in the hot Palestinian sun, and those three lonely birds in verses 6–7), the psalmist is confident of the salvation brought by the benign face of the Lord.

What, then, does the central part contribute to this theme? The re-establishment of Jerusalem after the exile is used as a metaphor for the re-establishment of the psalmist after this dire sickness. If the Lord can and will set up Jerusalem once more to be at the head of the nations and receiving their homage, he can and will also restore the psalmist.

The most intense and exciting section of the psalm is, however, the final one. There, the emphasis is on the transitory nature of the world: the heavens and the earth will perish, they will be changed, like a worn-out garment. And yet the Lord will be the same, and with him will be the psalmist, secure in his presence. At this stage of revelation, the final resurrection of the dead had not yet come into Israel's consciousness. There is, however, a proclamation of the belief that, when all is changed, when the universe itself has come to an end, God's faithful people will still be in the divine presence, standing before the face of the Lord.

3 The Lord forgives all your sins

Psalm 103 (102)

One could say that the whole psalter is a song of praise to the saving justice of God. That is certainly true of this psalm. It circles round the three ideas of forgiveness, loving mercy (*hesed*, considered in our notes a couple of psalms ago) and saving justice. These are the three aspects of God that are revealed as the Name of God in Exodus 34, which make Israel cling doggedly to God.

Saving justice was considered extensively in the commentary on Psalm 7 (*Guidelines May–August 2010*), but there is room for more! There is no concept in English that adequately renders this aspect of God. For lack of a better word, it is sometimes rendered 'righteousness', which at any rate shows that there is no normal English word for it, though it has the disadvantage of smelling of 'self-righteousness'—not an amiable quality. The reflection on Psalm 7 centred on God's own righteousness— that is, God's absolute fidelity to his promises, the ground of all human hope. What about human righteousness?

In the New Testament, the paradigm cases come in the infancy narratives. In Matthew 1:19, Joseph is called 'righteous'. In Luke's infancy narrative, all the principal actors are 'righteous': the parents of John the Baptist, Simeon and the parents of Jesus are equally eager to obey the law to the letter (Luke 1:6; 2:22–25). They are being shown to us as the final spearhead of the faithful of the Old Testament, putting all their trust in God and all their hope in the coming of his Messiah. Their guiding principle in life is to stay close to God's law, for to obey the law is a loving response to God's gift of his revelation and friendship in the law. The law shows human beings how to stay close to God, how to be God's people, living in the image of God. So, just as God's 'righteousness' is his fidelity to his promises made to Abraham, so human 'righteousness' is fidelity to God's way of life, revealed in the law. It is not a 'hard' concept, like 'self-righteousness' or 'zeal', but is a 'soft' concept, a gentle and generous concept of self-giving. One is tempted to translate it as 'devotedness'. The parents of John the Baptist and of Jesus, and all who were ready to welcome the Messiah, were devoted.

In praising the 'righteousness' of God, then, we pronounce our reliance on God's fidelity to his promises and yearn to be, ourselves, faithful to the gift of his guidance.

4 Wrapped in light as in a garment

Psalm 104 (103)

This is possibly the favourite of the creation psalms, rivalling Psalm 8 as the most beloved of the hymns of praise for the wonders and intricacy of God's creation. It shares many features and even verses with the Egyptian 'Hymn to Creation' (or 'Hymn to the Sun') attributed to Pharaoh Akhenaton, though direct borrowing in either direction is difficult to establish. It rejoices in the beauty and variety of created nature, including (vv. 16–18) such wonderful local features as the majestic cedars of Lebanon towering from the mountains, the delicate ibex or mountain goats (they blend so perfectly into the sandy rock of the wadis that they pass unnoticed till a stone is dislodged and tinkles down the slope) and the timid but inquisitive hyrax or 'rock rabbits' (not rabbits at all, but small, tailless, beaver-like creatures that bask in the sun and scuttle for safety in the rocks). Equal attention is paid to the young lions, who wait for darkness before they creep forth and roar for their prey, seeking their food from God (v. 21).

The series follows the order of the first creation narrative in Genesis 1 —a logical ordering, never intended as an historical, day-by-day account. First comes the framework—the light and the heavens—next the solid earth (v. 5), the springs of water that penetrate it from below and the rains from above (v. 10). Then come the moving things in the sky (v. 12), on earth (v. 20) and in the sea (v. 25), even the sea monsters which the Lord made to play with (v. 26).

The psalm concludes, as it began, with the praise of the Lord, leading the theme back to the beginning of the creation with the glory of the Lord, who is clothed in majesty. It has been suggested that Genesis 1 is a hymn to the one Creator, deliberately countering ideas that sun, moon and stars are gods in their own right: they are all the creatures of one God, planted by God in the heavens. In this psalm, too, sun and moon have their function within God's creation: the moon is merely a marker for feast days, and even the sun knows the time prescribed for its setting (v. 19). The psalm combines a reverence and affection for the things of earth with overwhelming praise for the Creator of them all.

5 Make known his deeds among the peoples

Psalm 105 (104)

There are two striking aspects to this historical psalm. The first is that there is no hint of the disobedience of Israel or the corrections meted out by God; the second is that it is centred on the covenant, not with Moses but with Abraham.

Most of the historical psalms are well aware of the chequered history of Israel's fidelity to God. So Psalm 78 (77) presents Israel as 'a defiant and rebellious race' constantly rebelling and deserting the Lord throughout its history. Psalm 106 (105) dwells on Israel's forgetfulness and idolatry. Not so Psalm 105, for all is calm and peaceful here. Joseph is merely the successful precursor of the chosen people going into Egypt. The oppression in Egypt is mentioned only to explain the plagues. Of these, a luscious account is given, considerably different from the account in Exodus, though the psalm's poetic form makes it hard to discern whether the underlying historical facts were different. The journey through the desert sees every desire of Israel fulfilled. At every step, the Lord is arranging history to Israel's advantage, to which Israel responds blamelessly. Water from the rock, manna and quails are all answers to Israel's prayers.

Secondly, the central figure is Abraham at both beginning and end (vv. 6, 9, 42). Normally, 'the covenant' immediately evokes the covenant made with Moses during the exodus, but here (as in Paul's meditation on Abraham's faith in Romans 4) the emphasis is on the ultimate father of the race. The return to the promised land is seen as the fulfilment of the promises made to him in Genesis 12. Not surprisingly, after this smooth and harmonious account of the partnership between God and Israel, the purpose of the whole history is delineated as the observance of God's precepts and laws (v. 45).

The stress on instruction, wisdom and the law shows that this is a Wisdom psalm, and should be regarded not only as a song of praise for God's direction of history in favour of Israel but also as a means of instruction. This makes it all the more remarkable: Wisdom literature dates from a late period in the history of Israel, and yet the singer of this psalm takes one small segment of the history of Israel, seeing in it God's benevolent conduct of Israel's history and Israel's unhesitating obedience.

6 Visit me with your saving power

This is the last psalm of Book Four, so the final verse should be seen as a doxology not to the psalm but to the whole book—as at the end of each of the five books. The psalm was no doubt put here as a companion to the previous psalm, teaching in a complementary way the lessons of God's actions in history.

Indeed, it stands in sharp contrast to the previous psalm. There Israel was quietly cooperative with the Lord; here the repeated rebellion of Israel is foremost. So the psalm begins and ends with praise of God, but it is the praise of God's forgiveness and mercy, his *hesed*, despite Israel's rebelliousness. Despite the threats of enemies and the infidelity of Israel, God is a God who saves, for God is a Saviour-God, and it is only in the course of the development of Christology that the title of Saviour is transferred to our Lord and Saviour, Jesus Christ.

There are two sharply distinct ways of looking at the Israelites' 40 years in the desert. One is as the ideal time of the honeymoon between Israel and her Lord, a time of peace and fidelity, an idyll of untrammelled love. We see this affection portrayed in Hosea 11:1–4: 'I called my son out of Egypt… I was leading them… with leading-strings of love… I was like someone lifting an infant to his cheek.' Jeremiah speaks of 'the affection of your bridal days' (Jeremiah 2:2). Another viewpoint is represented by this psalm—the continual complaint and murmuring of the people as they worked their way through that inhospitable desert, their failure to understand the wonderful deeds of God in Egypt, their defiance at the Red Sea, their impatience, greed and challenge to God in the desert, their disbelief in God's guarantee of a land, their provocation to God at Meribah, and their refusal to destroy the non-Yahwistic inhabitants of Canaan.

The desert of Sinai is indeed a testing place. Nothing grows in those vast expanses of harsh and unyielding sand. Of water, life and movement, there is nothing. Even the wild camels are panting in the merciless sun. To be lost on Sinai, as bewilderment passes to fear and frustration, is an experience that can still chill the heart years later. And yet, in this country of extremes, the brooding, unseen, almighty power of God is dauntingly present.

Guidelines

Several of the psalms in this group are reflections on God's guidance of the history of Israel and the ever-changing reaction of Israel to this guidance. This is surely one of the motives for belief in God and the destiny of Israel. The circumstances of the Israelites were extraordinary, from the special intervention of God to provide an heir to Abraham and Sarah in their old age onwards. The people of Israel were saved from disappearance by the planting of Joseph in Egypt to provide them with an anchorhold. Then they were rescued from destruction in Egypt, when they had so thoroughly given up hope that they could not even help themselves and pleaded to return to the 'leeks and onions' of Egypt. The wanderings in the inhospitable desert of Sinai turned out to be a source of strength to them. They settled in Canaan in the midst of a stronger civilisation, and their survival of the Philistine threat was turned to their advantage by the appointment of a king. The thread of fidelity was barely maintained despite all the materialistic temptations of the monarchy. When they had to be corrected by the exile to Babylon, they were still upheld by the promise of a new heart and a new spirit. The Christian view of Old Testament history as a painstaking preparation by God for the coming of his Messiah is surely justified.

21–27 January

1 Rescued by the Lord

Psalm 107 (106)

The structure of this psalm is beautifully neat and tidy. The three-verse introduction begins with the favourite reminder of the everlasting mercy of the Lord, before acclaiming his mercy in bringing together a people from the four corners of the world. What is this 'gathering' that is described in verse 3? The date of the psalm makes little difference to its meaning and impact. In the post-exilic era there were three pilgrimage-festivals of the year, and the psalm could refer to any of these gatherings, witnessing to the redemptive power of the Lord.

There follows the first main part of the psalm, which is composed of four neat and graphic sections on rescues from impending disasters, each with a parallel structure: a succinct and vivid description of the disastrous need, the cry for help, the rescue and the thanksgiving. In each, the desperate situation is sketched in a few well-chosen and deft strokes. The first describes one of the basic terrifying biblical experiences, and the desperate cry for help in a situation where there is no hope (vv. 4–9): no one who has not been lost in the desert can really understand the Bible. The second plunges into the filth, darkness and chains of primitive imprisonment (none of the humanitarian mitigations of the modern prison here) and the release for which there is no hope (vv. 10–16). The third vividly describes the powerless loathing of the sick (vv. 17–22). While it is being suffered, any illness seems irremediable and hopeless! The fourth (vv. 23–32) confronts the mighty power of the sea, with people being tossed around in a cockleshell boat. The people of the Bible were not natural seafarers, and their fear of the sea was intensified by their mental image of the earth, tucked into the middle of raging waters that threatened to engulf the whole if God should for a moment cease to restrain them. This fourth rescue leads not merely to a prayer of thanks but to a public thanksgiving in the open assembly.

These detailed rescue operations by the Lord are followed by a more generalised reflection (vv. 33–42) on God's habit of reversing situations—what might be called by Christians 'the Magnificat syndrome'—the power to humble the proud and exalt the lowly. This is imaginatively focused on the disconsolate prince, wandering alone in trackless wastes, contrasted with the rescued needy, gleefully tucked up at home, surrounded by a family as numerous as a flock.

2 'My heart is ready' and a curse of curses

Psalms 108 (107) and 109 (108)

The combination of parts of two other psalms creates a new prayer. Psalm 108 (107) is composed of Psalm 57:8–11 followed by Psalm 60:4–12. Each half of the psalm is torn from its context of a threatened situation and joined to the other, to make an altogether cheerful and positive hymn of praise.

An occasional prayer for vengeance occurs in several psalms, but never anything so sustained and prolonged as the curse in Psalm 109 (108). Attempts have been made to sanitise it, supposing that the main prayer against the persecutors (vv. 6–19) is a quotation by the psalmist of the persecutor's prayer against him, which is then summed up in the 'thus' of verse 20. However, this really is not justified by the wording and, in any case, does not succeed in its objective, for the psalmist, instead of exercising a nice Christian forgiveness, calls down the same curse on his tormentor!

It is better to accept that this is a really comprehensive, systematic and finely constructed curse. The enemy is to be condemned and his plea for mercy is to make matters worse. He is to lose his livelihood and life itself. His family, now widow and orphans, is to be torn apart and his property sequestered, his very name blotted out from the records. Not content with the condemnation of the enemy and his children, the curse spreads back up the line to his father and mother, so that their names too are blotted out and only their sin remembered. In a world to which the belief in eternal life had not yet penetrated, the continuance of the family name was all-important; yet this too is to be eradicated, and only a negative memory, the sin of the parents, is to remain. Cursing is to be not merely like clothing stuck to his body, but is to penetrate deep within him.

Standards of politeness, criticism, political correctness and vituperation vary from age to age. The fierce denunciations of John Chrysostom ('John the Silver-mouthed') against the Jews or Thomas More against Protestants make uncomfortable and unacceptable reading by today's standards. Even the gentle and shrinking prophet Jeremiah can be roused to ferocity against his tormentors: 'Hand their sons over to famine... Let their wives become childless and widowed. Let their husbands die of plague, their young men be cut down by the sword' (Jeremiah 18:21).

Perhaps it is better to luxuriate in the artistry of the curse and to remember that Old Testament morality merely limited vengeance to the measure of the original offence: 'an eye for an eye and a tooth for a tooth'. The total exclusion of all revenge comes only with the command of Jesus to forgive 70 times seven times. Fully half of Matthew 18, on the community, is occupied with the teaching on forgiveness, and forgiveness is the one petition of the Lord's Prayer that is repeated for emphasis immediately after the prayer. Let one who is without fault cast the first stone.

3 The Lord's revelation to my Lord

Psalm 110 (109)

For Christians, this psalm is unique. It is the psalm most often quoted in the New Testament, for it is seen as a direct prophecy of the kingly and priestly rule of the Davidic Messiah, seated at the right hand of the Lord. It makes use of the ritual of the priest-king of Jebusite Jerusalem, who appears in Melchizedek (whose name means 'my king is justice') in Genesis 14, and again in another king of Jerusalem, Adonizedek ('my lord is justice'). This same ritual hymn must have been taken over by David when he captured Jerusalem and made it his capital. The psalm is articulated on the two solemn promises of the Lord to the king. The first three verses celebrate the king's rule, and the next four his priesthood, both conferred by God's irrevocable oath. The text, particularly of verse 3, is thoroughly corrupt; but, however it is read, it celebrates the eternal divine origin and destiny of the king.

The promise that the king will be seated at the right hand of God is quoted in Peter's speech at Pentecost to prove the resurrection and exaltation of Christ (Acts 2:34), and again by the writer to the Hebrews to illustrate the eternal and overwhelming rule of Christ (Hebrews 1:13). There is a reference to it also in Jesus' reply to the high priest at the Jewish Sanhedrin hearing, when he declares that he is Messiah, Son of God and Son of Man, sharing God's throne and coming on the clouds of heaven (Mark 14:62). This is the moment in the Gospel when his identity is at last revealed. Finally it lies behind the great final scene of the book of Revelation, in the new Jerusalem, centred on God and the Lamb, when all creatures venerate *him* (not *them*) on *his* throne—a single divinity.

The second promise is the basis of the theology (especially in the letter to the Hebrews) of Christ's priesthood—a new priesthood, no longer the Old Testament, passing priesthood, but the eternal priesthood of Melchizedek, who has no beginning and no end. The risen and glorified Christ, the Lamb standing as though slain, presents his sacrifice once and for all time to the Father for the reconciliation of the human race.

The rather puzzling final verse is again a reference to the Jerusalem priest-king. When David's two sons, Solomon and Adonijah, were struggling for the succession to their dying father's throne, the determining factor seems to have been to draw living water from the only spring of Jerusalem, the spring of Gihon, which lies beside the road at the base of Jerusalem. It is this water that seems to confer legitimacy (see 1 Kings 1:33, 45).

4 I will praise the Lord with all my heart

Psalm 111 (110)

This is the first of two acrostic psalms, the initial letter of each line working through the Hebrew alphabet from beginning to end. This form seems to have been favoured in the post-exilic era, and the attachment of 'fear of the Lord' to Wisdom also suggests a late date.

It is a psalm of praise, beginning and ending with the thought of praising the Lord. In between, the subjects chosen may be dictated as much by the strict acrostic formula as by any other logic. The psalmist's thought seems to circle round the formative period of the Israelites in the desert of the exodus, when God ransomed them from slavery (v. 9), gave them manna for food (v. 5), formed the covenant with them (vv. 5, 9), and eventually displaced foreign nations for them (v. 6). More striking than this, however, is the constancy of God's care for his people: the word 'for ever' occurs in verses 3, 5, 8, 9 and 10. God's unflagging care is seen less in the particular elements mentioned—his works, his righteousness, his strength and his mercy—than in the whole structure of life. Although the historical context of the psalmist's thought is the exodus, the covenant made at that time in the desert continues 'for ever' to be the basis of Israel's life. There is a timelessness about the Torah, for it means not only the Book of the Law but, more widely, all the teaching about God and God's ways with the world. The mention of 'wisdom' in the final verse underlines this thought, for the fear of the Lord is the beginning of the covenant and the Torah, no less than of wisdom. 'To fear the Lord is the beginning of wisdom' is simply a more modern way of putting the matter.

The stability and comprehensiveness of the acrostic form, running from *aleph* to *tau*, or from A to Z, gives the psalm an inclusive and satisfying quality. It is a general psalm of praise and thanksgiving, about nothing in particular and yet about all God's dealings with his people. For the Christian, however, the concluding mention of wisdom must bring it to a climax, through the Pauline teaching that Christ himself is the power and the wisdom of God (1 Corinthians 1:24), not to mention the rather quirky insistence that Christ was the rock that followed the Israelites in the desert of the exodus and gave them water (1 Corinthians 10:4). It was Christ who accompanied them as that rabble of runaway slaves was being formed by their experiences into the people of God.

5 Blessed the man who fears the Lord

Psalm 112 (111)

This is the psalm for the successful businessman! There is no getting away from the materialist emphasis of the Bible: prosperity is a blessing from the Lord. Abraham was blessed with such increase of flocks and herds that he and his nephew Lot were compelled to split up to find enough grazing. After all his trials, Job was blessed with herds to make the mind boggle—6000 camels alone. Since healthy eating and gym clubs were still a fad of the future, to be unashamedly fat was a sign of divine favour.

There are, of course, two other essential dimensions to this blessing of success—justice and generosity. Justice is emphasised three times in the psalm, once with the word that really means 'straightforwardness' or 'fair dealing' (*yashar*), once with a more legal term suggesting discernment and fair judgment (*mishpat*) and once with the more comprehensive term (*zedaqah*) that almost means 'holiness'. The second essential element is generosity, mentioned twice in the psalm. There is no more room for close-fistedness than for crooked dealing.

Alongside the insight that wealth is a blessing of the Lord sits the somewhat paradoxical insistence that it is the poor, impoverished and oppressed who are the Lord's favourites. This idea is never absent from the Bible, visible in the earliest stories of desert hospitality (Abraham entertaining the three strangers, and his servant entertained by Rebekah, in Genesis 18 and 24), and the care in so many prescriptions of the law itself to protect the weak, widows and orphans. It comes to the fore especially with the experience of destitution in the Babylonian exile, when the Lord's favour becomes focused on the poor, the first recipients of salvation: 'Seek the Lord, all you humble of the earth' (Zephaniah 2:3).

In the Gospels we see it especially in Luke, where the poor and disadvantaged welcome the Saviour: no wise men bearing gold and costly spices, but empty-handed, threadbare shepherds come to the newborn displaced person, whose parents cannot afford the full sacrifice in the temple. Warnings of the danger of wealth culminate in the parable of the rich fool who builds himself new barns but has no time to enjoy his wealth (Luke 12:16–21), and a contrast is shown in the story of the centurion whose generosity wins him the cure of his servant (7:1–10). The psalm reminds us that there is no shame in success, but that it does bring its grave responsibilities.

6 To the childless wife he gives a home

Psalm 113 (112)

This psalm begins 'Hallel' or 'Praise!' It opens the group of psalms known as 'the Egyptian Hallel' from its concentration on the deliverance from Egypt (not especially evident in this first psalm). Psalms 113—114 were sung at the beginning of the Passover Seder, with the first cup of wine.

The psalm has three clear stanzas. The first is an enthusiastic exhortation to praise God, four times repeating the invitation, with an additional 'May the name of the Lord be blessed'. The second and third stanzas, in classic style, give the reasons for praise. The first of these two is praise of the Lord, exalted in the heavens and having complete control of the world from the sweeping dome of the heavens. Only at the end of the stanza comes the specific reason for this concentration on the heavens: God's height in the vast heavens brings out the contrast with his descent to the depths to lift up the lowliest of the lowly.

So we have the same theme—the Lord's care for the disadvantaged and those who humbly trust in him—as we saw in the previous psalm. The concentration this time is on the childless, who in some cultures are considered the most deprived of all people. In Africa, celibate clergy and religious, no matter how comfortably placed they are in material terms, are considered by their childlessness to have given up everything worthwhile. The same has always been true in Judaism, where man and woman were explicitly told to increase and multiply as a part of human nature as it was created by God (Genesis 1:28). In these circumstances, celibacy (where it is maintained) is a strong witness to the overwhelming value of the kingdom of God.

Thus it is apt that the final verse of the psalm repeats the core verse of the thanksgiving song of the supposedly barren Hannah, when she has at last given birth to her son, Samuel (1 Samuel 2:5). In the Bible there is a whole series of women who seemed destined to remain childless, only to be rescued from childlessness by divine intervention, as part of the plan of salvation history and evidence of God's greater plan: Abraham's wife Sarah, Samson's mother, and Elizabeth the mother of John the Baptist.

Guidelines

This highly diverse group of psalms leads to a reflection on how the psalms were gathered together and how they were used in the temple. We simply do not know. We know that some of them, like Psalm 113 (112), were used in the celebration of family festivals, but of their wider liturgical use we know nothing. The Psalms of Ascent (to which we shall shortly be coming) were presumably used by pilgrims going up to Jerusalem. Some of the psalms themselves suggest a refrain to be sung in response; some presuppose instruments—the clash of cymbals or fanfare of trumpets. The later superscriptions of others bear the name of a tune or a group of singers. Some celebrate a public victory or lament a national defeat. But what of the more private psalms? Was there a store of them on which the worshipper could draw at request? Were they all known by heart and stored in the memory for an occasion suitable to each? All we know is that they were the prayers of Israel, and we can only guess the details of their use. If we know them well enough, we will certainly always find a psalm to fit the needs of our prayer life.

Luke 14—17

Luke's Gospel is intimately linked to his second volume of the story—the Acts of the Apostles. His preface (Luke 1:1–4) indicates his purpose to give a well-researched and orderly (not necessarily chronological) account of Jesus' life and ministry. Chapters 14—17 recount part of the journey of Jesus to Jerusalem (for more on this theme, see *Guidelines January–April 2011, pp. 22–29*), a journey that begins with the transfiguration and ends with the crucifixion and resurrection.

Luke is noted for his gift of storytelling, and this section contains some of the best-known examples of parables unique to his Gospel, such as the prodigal son and the rich man and Lazarus.

Luke had a particular interest in meals, which are a strong feature in these chapters, occurring not only in the parables but also in descriptions of events in Jesus' life. Another interesting feature is the way in which Luke indicates Jesus' 'audience'. Although his listeners include the crowds, they are more often his disciples and, most frequently, the scribes and Pharisees (those who find Jesus a difficult challenge). Probably these encounters, instructions, explanations and parables were recognised by Luke's hearers as being relevant to them in different ways. The passages addressed to the scribes and Pharisees would help them to handle conflicts being encountered by the early church, while the passages addressed to the disciples would assist the Christians in their own development.

Always present, however, sometimes in the background and sometimes explicitly, is the sense of movement towards Jerusalem, which would be so decisive for the ministry of Jesus and then for the young church community as it undertook Jesus' ministry after his ascension. The conflicts intensify; Jesus' attempts to prepare the disciples for his death are threaded through the narrative, along with the call for his disciples to be ready to commit everything to Jesus.

There is, therefore, much to challenge us here about our discipleship and our mission today.

1 Sabbath lunch

Luke 14:1–6

This passage contains one of the key motifs that bind Luke's Gospel together: meals. The meals are of two main kinds: there are real ones, as here, and there are meals within parables, which we shall encounter in a few sessions' time.

Among the real meals, there are some that appear in other Gospels as well as Luke, such as the feast following the call of Matthew/Levi (Matthew 9:9–13; Mark 2:13–17; Luke 5:27–32) and, of course, the Lord's supper (Matthew 26:20–29; Mark 14:17–25; Luke 22:14–23; John 13). In addition, there are several that are specific to Luke, including meals with Simon the Pharisee (7:36–50) and Martha and Mary (10:39–42). These meals often lead on to some kind of controversy or conflict, as is the case here in Luke 14.

The probable context is that Jesus had been speaking at the synagogue: it was customary for the speaker to be invited for a meal. The note that this Pharisee was a 'leader' might suggest that the setting is Jerusalem, as might the ominous words 'they were watching him closely' (v. 1)—but this isn't conclusive because we know that people could be sent out from Jerusalem to question and trap Jesus. It is clear that Jesus could never relax: like today's celebrities and, indeed, ministers and Christian leaders, he was always in the spotlight.

The conflict is stimulated by the tension between the needs of a sick person and the 'requirements' of sabbath observation. In some ways, this encounter parallels Jesus' meeting with the man whose right hand was withered (6:6–11). Rabbinic and other texts suggest that there was considerable debate among the Pharisees as to the proper interpretation and application of the sabbath command, and Jesus' question in verse 3 exploits that debate. It is important to note two things. First, there is no indication that Jesus was intending to deny the validity of the sabbath command; indeed, his frequent presence at the synagogue suggests the opposite. Second, Jesus always apparently gave priority to the needs of the person in such situations. I say 'apparently' because these conflicts also involved facing, and not avoiding, the challenge with the leaders. His confrontations with both kinds of evil—the disease and the opposition from the religious officials—would contribute to his death.

2 Honour and shame

Luke 14:7–11

The encounter we studied yesterday left Jesus' opponents shamed: 'they could not reply to this' (v. 6). In such a debate, silencing your opponent was the equivalent of disarming your enemy in a medieval combat. The second incident that Luke sets in the context of this meal is also to do with honour and shame. For Westerners, however, the deep significance of this concept is difficult to appreciate truly.

With the healing of the man in yesterday's passage, the initiative for the conflict lay with the lawyers and Pharisees: Jesus' question in 14:3 was prompted by his realisation that they were 'watching him closely'. Here, however, Jesus takes the initiative, unprovoked. He notices some guests seeking out the best places—that is, positions nearest to the host and to himself as the chief guest. We can sometimes get a flavour of this in the organisation of wedding banquets, when we need to cope with anxieties over the seating plan and who should be on the 'top table'. The importance of this issue in Jewish society can be gleaned from references to Jesus being seated at the right hand of the Father (Acts 2:33), or the desire of James and John for the positions immediately to Jesus' right and left (Mark 10:37). It wasn't only about being seen; it was also about receiving rewards and the opportunity for further enhancement.

This passage is fascinating because it provides a rare glimpse into the way Jesus' parables could arise from particular and specific contexts. His 'story' is prompted by his observation of those around him. So he challenges them to explore humility and honour.

Whereas yesterday's passage centred on conflict to do with the law, here Jesus is appealing to proverbial wisdom: 'For it is better to be told, "Come up here", than to be put lower in the presence of a noble' (Proverbs 25:7). It is, however, possible that there is another level of challenge, as the same proverb begins by saying, 'Do not put yourself forward in the king's presence' (25:6). In common with the parables generally, there may be a covert meaning here for those 'with eyes to see and ears to hear'. The real host at this meal is not the 'leading Pharisee'; it is the hidden Messiah on his way to Jerusalem.

3 True hospitality

Luke 14:12–15

Jesus was deeply discerning. The guests who had been shuffling and pushing to get to the best seats had experienced the incisiveness of Jesus' observations, and it is not too difficult to think of contemporary parallels in the life of the church and the wider culture. But Jesus' discernment was not limited to the guests in front of him: it embraced the host beside him—a *leading* Pharisee! To emphasis the point that this was not a comment for the guests, the text notes, 'Jesus said to his host' (v. 12). Leaders too have their prevailing and revealing attitudes and actions.

There is a natural tendency for us all to invite the people who are closest to us—those we feel comfortable with, friends who share our values, close family (perhaps because it's a social requirement)—or wider family members whose contacts are likely to prosper us, or those with prestige or resources of wealth and reputation. Putting on a meal, for Jesus' hearers, was a costly and time-consuming affair. It had to be done well—exceedingly well—or their reputation would sink. So they didn't want to squander the opportunity: it was a cultural investment, a chance to enhance their honour in the community. The honour (and the investment) was doubled because they could expect to be invited back, so their reputation would then be enhanced by that of their host.

Reward for investment! It is so easy to allow calculations of cost and benefit to determine a guest list. What Jesus does by saying, 'Invite the poor, the crippled, the lame, and the blind' (v. 13: note the four categories, paralleling the list in verse 12) is to reveal and challenge the basis of the invitation and, alongside it, the nature of the 'meal event'. Jesus indicates that 'the banquet' (notice how the lunch or dinner has now become a banquet), rather than being a matter of reputation-building or investment, is meant to be an offer of hospitality, grace and generosity. If we act to promote these qualities, we reveal that we are like our Father in heaven. Jesus does not, I would suggest, tell this parable to accuse his host but to invite him to enter the kingdom—to explore his own heart by examining his own procedures.

4 Invitations

Luke 14:15–21

Jesus initiated the previous two conversation topics; now one of the guests makes the running. The text tells us that the comment 'Blessed is anyone who will eat bread in the kingdom of God' (v. 15) was made on 'hearing this'. What it doesn't specify is what 'this' is. Obviously the natural link is to 'you will be blessed' in verse 14, but 'this' might include the previous conversation topic, where Jesus recalled a proverb that made reference to the king. Perhaps it was this that fused the ideas of blessing and kingdom in the guest's mind.

Jesus response is typical: it engages with the comment made but does not provide a clear-cut answer. Through the parable of the 'great dinner', he seeks to open up the guests' minds by involving them in the story being told. All the guests loved to be invited to significant meals; clearly, to be a guest at God's table, at the 'messianic banquet', would be the ultimate invitation.

The invitation process involved two stages—ascertaining the availability of potential guests and then, when the meal was ready, a call to the meal. The invited guests in the parable have all said 'yes' at the first stage, so their refusal at the second is extremely rude. They are not really providing reasons for their non-attendance but making up excuses.

The refusals are a dreadful humiliation for the host (hence his anger), but he outwits the rude guests by ensuring that every place is taken—first by the marginalised in their community (v. 21) and then even further afield. The host ensures that there will be no room for the initial guests. Indeed, it will appear as if they have been spurned in favour of the 'riff-raff', so the shame will rebound on them.

Whether the master's 'slave' provides us with a glimpse of Jesus' self-identity (see Philippians 2:7), and whether the two groups correspond to Jesus' mission first to his own people and then to the Gentiles, are contested issues. What cannot be contested, though, is the challenge to the guests to reconsider their response to Jesus. Through him they are being summoned to God's banquet. They must beware of lame excuses.

5 The real thing

Luke 14:25–27, 34–35

This passage moves outside the home where Jesus has been at rest and puts him back 'on the road', picking up the theme of Jesus' determination to go to Jerusalem to fulfil his calling (see 9:31, 51). Jesus is depicted here as being surrounded by 'large crowds' (v. 25). If the previous episodes show just how tough Jesus was with the Pharisees and the elite in society, verses 25–35 show that he was equally tough with everyone. The issues at stake are matters of life and death, only more so—affecting life in the age to come as well as this age.

The two sets of verses we are reading today seem to be intended as a pair of complementary images, with two parallel stories inserted between them to amplify the issues. The way Luke uses the mini-parable about the salt (vv. 34–35) is rather different from the way it is used in Matthew 5:13 but may help us see the implications more clearly. To make sense of it, we need to note that salt was used as a fertiliser. Both the reference to salt and the startling allusion to crucifixion (v. 27) raise the issue of authenticity in discipleship. Nothing and no one can come between a person and his commitment to Jesus: inauthentic disciples are not an option.

The three pairs of relatives in verse 26 provide us with an insight into the priorities within the Jewish community's hierarchy. First in importance came parents (Exodus 20:12), then immediate family (Genesis 2:24) and then the wider family. But instead of suggesting a fourth pair, Jesus shocks his hearers by bringing the focus back to each individual's 'life itself'. No one would have been in any doubt about the claim Jesus was making. To claim such a high level of commitment was possible only if he thought of himself as divine (see Exodus 20:1–6). (The use of the word 'hate' in verse 26, as is now well appreciated, is an Eastern way of indicating strongly that the 'hated' person or thing must take second place.)

The image of crucifixion (v. 27) was a truly horrific and vivid one, as crucifixion was an ever-present threat for the Jews under Roman occupation, and would be awaiting Jesus when he reached Jerusalem. An authentic disciple is one who has made an absolute choice to put Jesus first.

6 Because he's worth it

Luke 14:28–33

Superficially, these two sayings, one about building a tower and the other about a king engaging in a major conflict, seem exact parallels. They both emphasise the need to consider seriously the overall cost of taking on a challenge rather than rushing into precipitous and public action.

Initially, the plan to build (probably a watchtower to be used for guarding crops against wild animals and thieves) seems both sensible and exciting. Equally, for a king who learns that a major invasion force is approaching his territory, the adrenalin will kick in, as well as pride and a desire to protect his territory, possessions and people. So he summons his army with all the cheers of the populace ringing in his ears!

Both pictures reinforce Jesus' point about authentic discipleship: it is not just about initial enthusiasm; it is about truly costly long-term commitments. It is one thing to join the crowds on a day's walk towards Jerusalem, as if it were a pilgrimage of the sort that Psalm 122 conveys, with everyone in a mood of elation. (This psalm, with its references to towers, relatives and friends, the temple and 'the peace of Jerusalem', may have been in Jesus' mind as he told the parable.) It is quite another thing to know that you are committed to travelling all the way to Jerusalem, there to be crucified. Jesus wants people to choose the long walk.

As we look a little closer at these two sayings, however, interesting variations emerge. 'Building a watch tower' would have been a relatively common experience for Jesus' hearers. Although only land owners would be expected to foot the bill, many would help in the construction or watch it happening. So Jesus begins by enfolding everyone into the story: 'For which of you…' (v. 28). The shame of failure would remain for all to see, bringing shame on the owner.

The second story has a more distant subject (a king), and the event described is a much rarer occurrence—invasion, as if by the Roman army—with consequences that are more cataclysmic. The king cannot avoid making a decision: the foreign army is approaching. It is better to surrender ('ask for terms of peace', v. 32) than to be assassinated. So Jesus, having involved the hearers through the first story, now indicates both the imminence and the life and death nature of the decision—to follow Christ or not.

Guidelines

These verses are a challenge to us all about the quality of our discipleship and our commitment to the mission of Jesus, as opposed to the comfortable compromises we might make. They invite us to reflect deeply on issues of pride, honour and human egos—both our own and within the life of the church. They probe the kind of church we run (who is it really for?) and even those we invite on to our Facebook page.

For some of us, they challenge us to consider how we can open minds that have been closed by familiarity with God and the gospel, and whether storytelling could be a key component in this. And for all of us there is the requirement to examine the depth and authenticity of our discipleship.

1 Because they're worth it

Luke 15:1–10

Events like the death of Princess Diana and, more recently, investigations such as the Leveson Inquiry into illegal press behaviour underline the enormous pressure that celebrities, as well as ordinary people who become the focus of attention, are put under in our world. Technology makes our culture very different from Jesus', but this passage reminds us of the constant and invasive scrutiny that he endured. He was trapped between the attention of the tax collectors and sinners and the 'grumbling' of the Pharisees and scribes (v. 2). This grumbling was by no means simply a sign of 'grumpy old man' syndrome; it indicates that they were complaining, seeking to establish grounds to accuse Jesus and get rid of him.

So when the text says, 'So he told them this parable...', which of the two groups was its intended audience? Perhaps it is even more pertinent to ask ourselves the question, 'How are we hearing these familiar stories?' Does our response show that we are with the sinners or the Pharisees?

We may not be able to determine whether Jesus was addressing the Pharisees or the tax collectors, but there is no doubt about the heart of his message. Those people who feel as if they are outsiders, and lost, really matter to God because they belong to him. Like the distressed sheep or the lost coin, their true significance and value can be properly gauged only once we remember that they are God's pride and joy.

Sometimes today, Christian leaders can feel the same pressure that Jesus did. Do we focus our attention on the established believers or the 'tax collectors and sinners'? Perhaps church activities, including worship, are being reshaped to help those who are currently outside the church community, or resources are used to serve people beyond the church, or it appears that undue attention is given to those who are 'new'. Then we experience the challenge of Jesus' words for ourselves. But we can also hear the encouragement to fulfil his mission to those who (in the eyes of some established and respected Christians) seem to be lost or hopeless cases.

'There will be more joy in heaven over one sinner who repents than over ninety-nine righteous people who need no repentance' (v. 7). Clearly, divine responses are not strictly mathematical! How we respond to these issues is a good guide to how well we understand God's grace.

2 Death and renewal

Luke 15:11–24

Two short and parallel stories are followed by a third—often known as the parable of the 'prodigal son' or sometimes the 'waiting father'. This is probably the best-known and most preached on of all the parables, certainly of those that are specific to Luke's Gospel. It is exquisitely told and continues to capture people's imaginations today. Bible Society runs a short-film competition called 'The Pitch' and, every year, even though people can relate their film to any part of the Bible, out of fewer than 100 entries there are always several retelling this parable.

We are exploring these parables through the lens of the imagination more than that of critical scholarship (though both have their role to play). So we dwell on a simple verse: 'The younger one said to his father, "Father, give me my share of the estate"' (v. 12).

The question to ponder is what lay behind such an improper, even dangerous, request. It was dangerous because it was tantamount to wanting the father dead, thus breaking one of the Ten Commandments. Expulsion from the family, the home and the community could have been the outcome. In the West, with our experience and tolerance of teenage rebellion, we can consider this an extreme expression of the need for teenagers to find themselves and escape from parental control.

Some have noticed the absence of a mother or any other woman in this story. Had the mother died or had the father divorced her? Is a deep sense of loneliness the reason why the son feels the need to get away— because he cannot bear the pain of a lost mother? However, I favour the view that relates the demand for half the estate to the son's relationship with his older brother. It is not until the prodigal's return that we discover anything about the character of the older brother, but, once we do, many of us have considerable sympathy with the younger one's need to escape! This prompts a serious missional question for the churches and for each Christian. To what extent do our behaviour, our attitudes, our dress codes, our kinds of relationship and understanding and practice of Christian community contribute to the exodus of young people (as well as some older ones) from our churches? Research about why people leave churches suggests that those of us who stay have a lot to answer for.

3 Rejection

Luke 15:22–32

It appears that this parable has come to a fitting conclusion, precisely paralleling the previous two: 'So they began to celebrate' (v. 24). But then, amazingly, the story continues: 'Meanwhile, the elder son was in the field…' (v. 25)

If the first half of this extended story is affirming the tax collectors and sinners, those considered to be outside the true people of God, this second half is Jesus' appeal to the Pharisees and scribes.

Running throughout the passage is the theme of rejection. The older brother feels rejected by his father, because of the father's obsession with his wayward son. His bitterness festers and is exacerbated by the extravagant and socially unwarranted banquet given for the prodigal when he comes home. Thus his resentment is expressed in a similar framework: he rejects his brother, unable even to name him as his brother ('this son of yours', v. 30).

The older son's behaviour shows that he has rejected his father too. If he is indeed now his father's only son, it behoves him to treat his father with the utmost respect and courtesy, but in fact, when the father's appeal cuts across his own preferences, he brazenly refuses to comply: 'Then he became angry and refused to go in' (v. 28). He is insulting his father, just as the various guests did their host in Luke 14:15–21.

Unlike that host, however, the father refuses to reject his older son for his insolent behaviour. The same generous and undeserved embrace that the father extends to the 'prodigal' is also available for the older brother.

So Jesus invites the Pharisees and scribes to find themselves in this story. He hints at the lurking fears and prejudices they hold against others. Yet they could hear, if they had ears to do so, the love of God for them, the security that God offers them (v. 31). Will they accept God's appeal through Jesus, or will they continue in their obdurate rejection of the God who loves them?

These are questions not only for them but also for all of us who consider ourselves to be 'on the inside'. This parable compels us to step into the story. If we don't have the Father's heart for the lost, do we have the Father's heart at all?

4 The real challenge of the dishonest manager?

Luke 16:1–12

Do cryptic crosswords engage you? Do you enjoy solving really well-constructed and difficult crime novels? If so, this parable should appeal to you, but for most people it is a really tough challenge.

It's easy to be drawn into the flowing narrative and joyful outcomes of the parables in chapter 15, where we find ourselves approving the plot, but this one shouts at us, 'It's wrong!' The manager's behaviour is wrong—not simply the 'squandering' of his property' (v. 1) but, even more so, his devious plan of cancelling up to 50 per cent of the debts owed to the master. Most shocking of all, though, is the master's verdict on this behaviour: he 'commended the dishonest manager' (v. 8)!

How can such irresponsible behaviour be commended? We won't tolerate it in MPs' false expenses claims; benefit 'cheats' are surely not to be praised; city traders who gain huge bonuses at the expense of people's pension funds cannot expect society's adulation. The case Jesus describes seems pretty close to these.

We may even be familiar with some of the common explanations from recent decades, which go like this: 'Parables only make one point, so the details of the serious impropriety don't count. The real point is that because God's kingdom is imminent, any steps to be made right with God and so to be ready for his coming should be taken. What is being commended is not the (im)morality of the manager's dubious actions within the story, but only the fact that he was prepared to take decisive action appropriate to the seriousness of his position, because he accepted the certainty of his master's summons.'

Kenneth Bailey indicates that the truth is probably more complex, given the social context of the story (see *Poet and Peasant*, Eerdmans, 1976, pp. 86–110). Although the manager was fired, he was not jailed as he could have been. So, acting on his knowledge that the master is generous and merciful, the manager uses his remaining time in the job to negotiate a good deal for the tenants (so that they will treat him well) and the master cannot then touch his manager without losing face in the community. As Bailey puts it, 'Because the master was indeed generous and merciful, he chose to pay the full price for his steward's salvation' (p. 102). The real challenge is to live our ordinary lives, with all their complexities, in the light of the nature of a merciful God.

5 The Law

Luke 16:13–18

We often think that the New Testament's understanding of the relationship between Christians and the Jewish Law was shaped primarily by positive experiences such as Peter's encounter with Cornelius and the Holy Spirit (Acts 10), alongside the somewhat acrimonious debates hinted at by Paul in passages like Galatians 2 and the attempt to formulate some guiding principles at the Council of Jerusalem (Acts 15). These experiences and accounts certainly indicate that working out the relationship was a key challenge for the young Christian community, but today's passage is one among many in the Gospels which strongly suggest that it was a red-hot topic for Jesus and his disciples.

Almost each word of these verses requires a set of notes to itself, but we will consider just one point. Verse 16a may be translated in different ways: for example, 'The Law and the Prophets were proclaimed until John' (NIV); 'The law and the prophets were in effect until John came' (NRSV); 'The law and the prophets lasted until John' (Tom Wright, *Luke for Everyone*, p. 196). While these versions agree that John the Baptist made a significant difference, the implications of the change that he initiated are rather different. In fact, there is no verb supplied in the Greek of verse 16, so something has to be added, but what should it be?

The NIV's translation can be supported by the claim that John 'proclaimed the good news to the people' (Luke 3:18, NRSV). In other words, in John's call for repentance, the heart of the proclamation is no longer 'law and prophets' but good news—the good news of the coming Messiah and his kingdom. The NRSV's translation, '… were in effect until John', indicates that a different 'regime' was inaugurated by John's presence. It does not imply that the law and prophets no longer existed. Tom Wright's translation strongly suggests that the law and the prophets were finished with by the coming of John: they only 'lasted' until then. Perhaps, if 'the law and the prophets' is understood as a paraphrase for 'the Old Testament covenant', that makes it more comprehensible. This would make the interpretation similar to the NRSV's version.

Certainly the following verses (vv. 17–18) indicate that Jesus could not have meant that the Law ceased to have validity.

6 Making sense of 'the Law and the Prophets'

Luke 16:19–31

Like the previous passage, this parable and the history of its interpretation require a book to themselves. We are keeping our eye on the words that link it to the previous passage: 'Moses and the prophets' (vv. 29, 31). Not only does this phrase pick up on the theme of the previous verses and so warrant our attention, but from a literary perspective also it is presented as the climax and focus of the parable.

'If they do not listen to Moses and the prophets, neither will they be convinced even if someone rises from the dead' (v. 31). These are the words that reverberate around the hearers' minds when the speaking stops. It is properly pointed out that 'Moses and the prophets' is an alternative phrase to 'the law and the prophets', denoting the same thing. We can see something similar in Luke 24, where the same material is described as 'Moses and the prophets' (v. 27; see also v. 44, which adds 'the psalms') and as 'the scriptures' (vv. 32, 45).

Maybe there is a subtle difference, however. By using the name 'Moses' in place of 'the law', and adding the verb 'listen', this parable is probably making a subtle shift towards personalising the text. If they listen, the 'five brothers' (v. 28) may hear the personal testimony of Moses and the individual prophets (not just 'the law' as an impersonal narrative read out in the synagogue, for instance). This personal testimony, then, is not much different from hearing the testimony of a person who has been sent back from the dead.

The major point, however, is that the law and the prophets have validity as testimony to the reality of life in the kingdom (or, indeed, life outside the kingdom). Although, in the immediate context of this parable, the 'someone' who rises from the dead (v. 31) would be Lazarus, the text is open to being understood as pointing to John the Baptist (we know that there was such speculation around: see Luke 9:7) or, for Luke's readers, Jesus himself. Whilst initially it appears ironic that it took Jesus' resurrection from the dead to convince his disciples of his claims, the parable throws light on that—for it is through the testimony of 'Moses and the prophets', via the interpretation of Jesus, that they are convinced.

Guidelines

One of the most difficult challenges for church leaders today is that of dealing with 'mixed audiences'. The preacher may well be speaking to listeners who have absorbed the content of the Bible and sought to apply it over decades and, at the same time, those who are almost totally biblically illiterate and have nothing of the Christian ethos in their spiritual blood stream. There may be some whose faith is more traditional than personal, and some who have so recently come to faith that the intense intimacy of their relationship with Jesus may frighten or embarrass others. The same challenge is found across the life of the churches, from small groups to social care projects, from children's work to the music group.

In the early part of this week's readings, we saw Jesus addressing a 'mixed audience'. What can we learn from his approach to stimulate our thinking and practice in similar situations?

The three parables about being lost and found are among the best-loved and best-known of all Jesus' stories, and they resonate with our culture too. Please take time to 'dwell in the story': seek to allow the radical encouragements and challenges of these stories to penetrate the armour of familiarity, so that, as for Luke's church, they become God's word to you.

Only slightly less familiar is the parable of the rich man and Lazarus. One of the issues it raises is that of authenticating the Christian message. It contrasts personal (indeed, miraculous) testimony with the authority of scripture. Do you agree that if people won't accept the message of scripture, they won't recognise the validity of personal testimony? This seems counter to many experiences and views today. Does Jesus' approach apply only to those who are already steeped in the scriptures?

11–17 February

1 Sinners and sinned against

Luke 17:1–4

This passage indicates that it is not only 'the law' and 'the prophets' that take sin seriously (see, for example, Deuteronomy 27; Ezekiel 18; Amos

2:4–5), but so does the Christian community. Jesus is once again address-ing his disciples (after having spoken to the Pharisees in 16:14 onward).

Christian disciples need to be serious about their responsibility not to cause offence to others. 'Little ones' (v. 2) denotes young disciples here (see the equivalent Matthew 18:6, which adds the clarifying phrase 'who believe in me'), although the Gospels also emphasise Jesus' commitment to children and their need for special treatment.

If one disciple causes another to 'stumble', it will not do for the first to maintain, 'Well, it was bound to happen anyway.' Later in Luke, Jesus predicts that Satan will be testing the disciples and, indeed, that Peter will fail (see 22:31–34), but Jesus models what it means to care: not only does he alert Peter to the coming dangers but he adds, 'I have prayed for you.' Here in chapter 17, however, Jesus wants to alert the disciples to their responsibility not to cause others to stumble. He underlines it with the image of a dreadful end, both unavoidable and terrifying (v. 2: the Jews had a horror of the sea). Even this is to be preferred to facing God's judgment.

These words challenge us in our missional context, where behaviour that is acceptable and manageable for us personally might lead relatively new believers to stray and even abandon their faith (see Romans 14).

One way we can be implicated in someone's stumbling is by not hav-ing enough love, wisdom or courage to show them what is going wrong in their lives. By alerting them to the dangers of a particular pathway, we may be able to encourage them to stick with their commitment to follow Christ. Equally, however, we can also cause offence by refusing to forgive. If we refuse to welcome back those who slip into past sinful behaviour patterns or appear to give up on their faith, when they wish to return, we will be driving them away from God. We then become a living denial of God's gospel grace.

These words are a real challenge to churches that are effectively reach-ing into our secularised and morally desensitised communities. We must be ready to point out where people are going wrong but, at the same time, hold out to them the possibility of being forgiven by God.

2 Increase our faith

Does verse 6 support those who believe in and practise a positive 'prosperity gospel' approach to faith? According to this belief, as part of the whole gospel, God has promised not only to provide for our needs but also to bless us with superabundance. So then, it is appropriate to ask God for health, wealth and material possessions. If we have faith in the generosity and power of God, then we will ask and receive all we ask for. Those who accept the 'prosperity gospel' will see those of us who don't as people who lack faith in the greatness and goodness of God. Is it not a 'plain reading' of scripture to see in this verse an encouragement to expect prosperity from him?

It is worth noting that this and the similar sayings in Matthew 17:20 and Mark 11:22 are set in three very distinct contexts. For Matthew, it is Jesus' response to the disciples' concerned question as to why they couldn't 'drive out' a demon; in Mark it is part of Jesus' response to the bewilderment of the disciples when they see that the fig tree he cursed has withered; here in Luke, it seems to be in response to the disciples' appeal for help in continuing to forgive people who wrong them (compare also John 14:13–14).

This varied usage strongly suggests that it was recognised to be an important saying of Jesus, which the Gospel writers and their communities took very seriously and applied to several different types of scenario. A second observation is that in none of the contexts does the person who exercises (or is encouraged to exercise) the faith become the primary beneficiary of it. Additionally, all three outcomes to which this faith is related are signs of the inbreaking of the kingdom of God.

Probably, then, the faith that Jesus describes is not some kind of 'positive thinking', in which the outcome depends on our being totally convinced (a subjective confidence). Rather, it is a faith that recognises the inevitability of the coming of God's kingdom with Jesus (an objective confidence in God). This relates closely to the thinking of John 14:9–12, about having faith in Jesus. Anything that is aligned with the name of Jesus can be commanded. As Tom Wright puts it, 'It's not great faith you need; it is faith in a great God' (*Luke for Everyone*, p. 204).

3 A servant heart

Luke 17:7–10

Having the right attitude is so important to Jesus, and yet, so often, our society tells us it's only results that matter—whether that means winning football matches, making a profit, or even growing the church. By contrast, whether we are helping the vulnerable, giving alms or even praying face to face with God, as in the parable of the Pharisee and the tax collector (Luke 18:9–14), according to Jesus the clarity and direction of our heart are primary.

This cameo of a common situation would, presumably, have brought a smile to the disciples' faces. Some of them may even have had their own servants or slaves, and have had to deal with awkward ones like the ones hinted at here. It is hard for us to experience the immediate response that the story would have generated in the disciples because we are used to expecting our rights (including our lunch-breaks); we expect to be treated with respect, and, if we are not, there are complaints procedures. Abuse or bullying in the workplace is not to be tolerated. But for household slaves there was none of this. Even after a hard day in the burning sun, they had to get a meal ready for their master—and that was no quick fix. They would have to gather the fuel to heat the oven, grind the corn and milk the goat, as well as cooking and serving.

Even then, the slaves are expected to say, 'We have only carried out our duty!' The point Jesus is making is that God is never in our debt. We can never say to God, 'I've done all this for you, so you owe it to me to sort this problem out for me.' Such feelings betray, in the end, that we are serving our egos—or, if indeed we are serving God, then it is for self and not for love or for his glory.

Jesus, then, challenged the inappropriate attitudes that easily developed in the disciples, and he challenges such attitudes in today's disciples too. Surely, for our service, commitment, endeavour, sacrifice or loyalty we deserve proper recognition? Yes, it's nice to be thanked and it often helps us keep going, but, if we think such affirmation is our right, then we have got it all wrong. If this attitude could be a problem even for disciples in a slave culture, how much more for us, with our positive rewards and protected rights.

4 Another Samaritan

Luke 17:11–19

Probably the most famous Samaritan of all time was fictitious—the good Samaritan in Jesus' parable (Luke 10:25–37). Here we meet a real one with probably just as much claim to fame and an equally important lesson to teach us all.

This account is full of details that add to the sense of realism. Life was harsh for all ten of the lepers. They lived on the borders between Samaria and Galilee, between civilisation and the wilderness. Perhaps the reason for the location of the colony was that neither the Galileans nor the Samaritans could evict its inhabitants: they could slide across the border from one region to the other if the authorities came to clear them out. They were at the entrance to the village so that they didn't contaminate others (see Numbers 5:2–3) but this made them more vulnerable to robbery and the attacks of wild animals. They may have camped as near to the village as possible so that food and help could be brought out to them. Like urban foxes, they lived in the twilight zone.

Their address, 'Jesus, Master' (v. 13), is intriguing. Clearly, they managed to glean gossip, so they were able to recognise Jesus. The use of 'Master' is typically Lucan—the word he often uses for rabbi or teacher. The lepers' appeal for 'mercy' may simply indicate a request for alms, on the assumption that Jesus' band of disciples will be carrying supplies, or they may be recognising his divine authority and asking for God's help (see also 18:38–39; Acts 3:1–3). The latter is certainly what they got, although they may not have realised it immediately. Jesus' command 'Go and show yourselves to the priests' (v. 14) implies that they are healed, because that was what people with skin diseases were supposed to do when they thought they had been healed (Leviticus 13:1–8). Jesus often engages and develops people's faith by challenging them to do something rather than intellectually affirm something or feel something.

Unusually, the highlight of this miracle story is not the healing or any confession of faith in Jesus, but thanksgiving to God, focused on Jesus (see vv. 15–16). Beyond even this, however, is the affirmation of the Samaritan's response by Jesus (vv. 17–19). It is not nationality but the reality of grateful faith that counts.

5 The heart of the kingdom

Luke 17:20–25

In the next two sections we look at two points that are highly contested but also take us to the heart of the kingdom.

'The kingdom of God is among you' appear to be very simple words (only two in Greek). That is the NRSV's translation of verse 21, but a footnote adds an alternative to 'among', namely 'within'. In the early part of the 20th century, 'within' was the preferred translation. It seemed to chime well with a personal, individual and spiritual understanding of the kingdom of God. Christianity was about our interiority, our personal relationship with God, nurtured by our hearts. It was apolitical and did not depend on external rituals or community living, although it might extend to our thought world and even our moral behaviour.

From 1950 onwards, the popularity of 'among you' developed. Imagine Jesus surrounded by the Pharisees. 'The kingdom of God is among you' ('you' plural, not singular—that is, 'within you as a group', 'in your midst') is an implicit challenge to see Jesus, who is at centre of the group, as the one where the kingdom of God is to be found. Everything he does, in terms of healings and exorcisms (even gathering disciples and 'sinners'), is a valid sign of the kingdom.

This interpretation fits well with many other sayings of Jesus. It also chimes well with an ambiguity about the word 'observed' (v. 20). To observe means not only 'to look at with our eyes' but also 'to watch for in order to catch'. As in Luke 11:53–54, Jesus knows that the Pharisees are trying to trap him, but they cannot see the kingdom in front of their eyes. The heart of the kingdom is Jesus; belonging to the kingdom means following him, being part of the group of disciples who were also 'among them'.

A second insight about the heart of the kingdom has to do with the way it comes. Verse 11 told us that Jesus was 'on the way to Jerusalem'. Luke's account of the transfiguration, which takes place just before Jesus sets out on the Jerusalem road (9:28–35, 51), indicates that the events in that city were to mark a new exodus ('departure', 9:31), inaugurated by the death of the firstborn. Jesus reaffirms that it is suffering—his suffering—and not military might that marks the progress of the kingdom of God. This truth is not offered to the Pharisees, however—only to the disciples (see v. 22).

6 On that day

Most people have a longing to know the future—hence the popularity of fortune tellers and horoscope readers. We also long for the good times, so we plan our holidays in the middle of winter to give ourselves a lift. The Gospels show us how the disciples (and many of their contemporaries) combined both these traits; they wanted to know when the 'end of the age' or 'the day of the Lord' would come. For them, these normal human aspirations were intensified as they followed Jesus and sensed that he was the Messiah or the Son of Man—roughly speaking, the person who would bring in God's reordering of the world.

Jesus has just indicated that the kingdom of God is present with him (17:21). In these following verses, he picks up the theme of the unpredictability of God's restoration of the world order. It can't be discerned by human observation: the normal laws of prediction don't work with God's planning.

Perhaps Jesus is also contrasting the reality of the kingdom with the kind of 'signs' that were listed in contemporary apocalyptic literature—disturbances in the heavens, plagues on earth and so on. These were events that couldn't be missed, so they would serve as advance warnings. For Jesus, though, the coming kingdom is not something you can look for and then decide whether you like it or not. Nor can you work out its arrival time from the way humans are behaving (perhaps Jesus had in mind the fact that some animals seem to be alert to signs of an imminent earthquake or violent storm).

Jesus recalls two well-known incidents from the Jewish scriptures to make his point—the flood in the time of Noah (Genesis 7) and the destruction of Sodom and Gomorrah (Genesis 19). He seems to be emphasising the continuing normality of life and therefore the impracticality of thinking that we can wait until the end is about to happen before we prepare for it. It will happen suddenly (vv. 34–35) and comprehensively (v. 24).

In fact, the only way to be ready is by making and keeping a commitment to Jesus: 'Whoever tries to keep their life will lose it, and whoever loses their life will preserve it' (v. 33, TNIV). This closely echoes Jesus' earlier words in Luke 9:23–25, where the critical issue of allegiance to the Son of Man is more visible. The meaning is the same here: Jesus will suffer many things and be rejected, and so will those who want to be in the kingdom of God.

Guidelines

This week's readings present very different challenges to us from last week's, which were mainly parables. Here there are two key issues. The first is about the quality of our faith. The measure that Jesus uses seems to be related to attitudes, not Jewish orthodoxy. What is our attitude to those whose faith is less secure than ours, and how far are we willing to forgo our own pleasures and comforts to avoid hindering those fellow believers? Our answer is one indication of how much or little we are truly committed to Jesus. A similar test is that of the limits we place on offering forgiveness.

Positively, can we exercise our faith in such a way that we show we recognise the ultimate victory of God's kingdom, but without distorting that victory into a mechanism for selfish advancement? Do we express our gratitude to God as vehemently as the healed Samaritan did, or are we like the majority who accept the gift of life and its many blessings as a right?

Secondly, where do we see the heart of the kingdom? Are we easily attracted by novelty and excitement in our faith journey? Or do we commit ourselves to the one who alone brings in the kingdom, even when the journey is ordinary or tough?

These challenging and penetrating questions encourage deep reflection, prayer and, perhaps, repentance.

FURTHER READING

I. Howard Marshall, *The Gospel of Luke* (New International Greek Testament Commentary), Paternoster, 1978.

Darrell L. Bock, *Luke* (New Testament Commentary Series), IVP, 1994.

Henry Wansbrough, *Luke* (People's Bible Commentary), BRF, 1998.

Tom Wright, *Luke for Everyone*, SPCK, 2001.

Environment

Last New Year, we went for a beautiful walk in the countryside with Sage, our local Christian environmental group. It was a fantastic day and the local countryside was glorious. There is a timelessness about nature and, looking around, we could be forgiven for thinking that all is well with the earth—but the environment continues to be in our news and, sadly, the reports are not good ones. In the last couple of years, Pakistan, Cambodia, Thailand, Burma and Australia have all experienced terrible floods, which have wiped out farms and washed people out of their homes. The result has been death, disease and hunger, with poor prospects for the future. Other parts of the world, such as the Horn of Africa, have been hit by drought and famine. These are weather impacts that we would expect to see if our climate were warming up, and the impacts are felt most strongly in some of the poorest parts of the world.

Climate change is not the only environmental problem that we face this century. In 2011, global human population possibly reached seven billion— five times what it was 100 years ago. We are seeing a huge decline in bio-diversity, especially through the loss of tropical forest cover. Water scarcity is becoming an issue worldwide. The supply of oil and gas is not going to keep up with global demand and there are some controversial methods being used to reach more difficult sources. So the natural world is in a sorry state. How do we understand this as Christians and how should we respond?

In the next two weeks we are going to explore a biblical basis for valuing and caring for creation. In the first week we will consider the Old Testament; the second week will focus on the New Testament and our relationship with nature from a gospel perspective. Overall, we will see how the Bible provides a fresh approach to tackling a number of contemporary problems. We will also look at some practical issues in our own lives, and finally we shall explore the Christian message of hope. This is vital for us and also for many people in the wider community who have lost confidence in the future.

Quotations are taken from the New International Version of the Bible.

1 A good creation

Genesis 1:1–25

The opening words of Genesis are majestic. The writer declares that God is before everything and that he created everything. Whatever the mechanism of creation, Genesis declares that it has its origins in a Creator God.

The word 'good' is used seven times in this chapter (seven being a symbol of perfection). God's creation is good—every bit of it. At different times in history, there have been debates over the goodness of the world. Some of the ancient Greek philosophers took a more negative view. Plato and some of his later followers, such as Plotinus, considered that goodness was only to be found in the higher spiritual realm. At different times in history, this thinking has led to a devaluing of our natural world, and, sadly, many Christians have absorbed it, wrongly believing it to be biblical Christian doctrine. Yet the biblical text challenges this view. The material world is made by God, and he saw it as good before humans were created. The value God places on each part of creation is shown by the careful way in which the different aspects of the cosmos and our own planet are described. Each part of creation therefore has value in its own right, and we should approach it with the view that it belongs to God and not ourselves.

Sometimes, when people want to put forward reasons for looking after the environment better, they suggest human reasons for doing so. For example, they will say that there may be is a cure for cancer in the biodiversity of a tropical rainforest. Although this is very important, we also need to value nature for its own sake, because our Creator God declared creation to be good before humans existed. The goodness of creation therefore depends on the value placed on it by God and not its usefulness to humans. Our universe is finely tuned for life, and our planet has just the right conditions for life. Atheists sometimes use the 'multiverse' theory to explain this: they suggest that there are an infinite number of universes and that we happen to live on the one where everything is finely and exactly set up to support life. Faith in God seems more straightforward!

2 Humans and nature

As Genesis 1 draws to a close, we see the creation of humans as the last stage of God's good creation. Here the attention turns to people—our food and our relationship with the rest of nature. Humans are commanded to be fruitful and fill the earth (v. 28). Does this sanction unlimited growth, or have we already fulfilled this commandment? Today our global food production depends heavily on nitrogen fertilisers, which are produced through the use of increasingly scarce fossil fuels. Much food goes to waste in the West, and land is not in full production. In poorer countries, the problems are often those of distribution and disruption through conflict. If we are to have a level of human population that can be sustained in the long term, we need to consider all these issues thoughtfully.

The command to 'subdue' the earth (v. 28) has been highlighted by those seeking to challenge the positive concept of biblical stewardship. The Hebrew word (*kabash*) literally means to 'tread down', but it is usually used to describe ploughing. Placed together with a command to reproduce, it provides a picture of humans farming the land to produce food for a growing family. We need to place this teaching alongside our study of Genesis 1:1–25. There should be a balance between adapting ecosystems for our own use and safeguarding nature because we recognise that it has value in its own right. How we can manage the balance of that relationship is explained as the biblical teaching on the environment unfolds.

The Hebrew word for 'rule' (*radah*) is a key concept in verse 28 (NIV), but it is also controversial. The NRSV follows the King James Bible, translating it as 'dominion', which might imply an exploitative rule over the natural world. However, we detect a different meaning once we know that the same word is used to describe Solomon's God-given rule over Israel (1 Kings 4:24). To 'rule', in biblical thinking, means to be given a responsibility. The rule of humankind should be life-giving rather than exploitative. Jesus demonstrates this in his ministry—for example, in Matthew 8, where he heals several people and calms a storm on the Sea of Galilee. In these miracles, he demonstrates his Lordship over creation.

Humanity has been given leadership over the rest of creation, as our very first responsibility. How well have we exercised it?

3 Rest and relationship

Genesis 2:1–15

Creation was not finished until the seventh day, when God created rest. Our beautiful world is full of complex cycles and changes of season, but rest is essential. God blessed this day of rest and made it holy. As we look at the financial crisis worldwide, we might reflect that a major reason why our world has slid into chaos is because we have ignored rest. Humanity has continued to use up resources without any thought of giving time to replenish stocks. Our economic system is based on the concept of continual growth, and yet our planet is finite. When we rest, our minds and bodies are restored and renewed. Rest periods are characteristic of all life on earth. Rest gives us the time to reflect on the other parts of our life. It is also a statement that we are content to have enough and not to work endlessly for more. We have worked our planet without rest, and the ecological crisis is a predictable result.

The text changes tone from verse 4, where we have a second account of creation, this time written in narrative form. We miss some of the nuance of this text in English translation. God forms human (*Adam*) out of the dust (*Adomah*). Literally, God creates us from earth and calls us 'earthy'. This implies a deep connection between humans and our earth. We are a part of this creation and not separate from it. We need to regain this truth in order to make good decisions about how we provide leadership for the biodiversity of the earth.

God then created a beautiful garden for humans to live in. He placed them in the garden 'to work it and take care of it' (v.15). These words are also important as we build a foundation for biblical creation care. The word 'work' (*avodah*) also means 'serve', and is used elsewhere to describe discipleship: we are called to love God and serve him with all our hearts and souls (Deuteronomy 10:12). The word translated 'take care of' is often translated as 'keep' (*shamah*) and is also found in the Aaronic blessing, 'The Lord bless you and keep you' (Numbers 6:24). In caring for the garden, we serve before the Lord and are called to care for it and protect it in the way that God cares for us. What a calling!

4 Called to the land and called to justice

Leviticus 25

In the opening sentences of Leviticus 25, there are two clear statements about human relationship with the land. First of all, the land is a gift of God: it belongs to him, not us. Secondly, we are called to respect limits and to have our sabbath rests, not simply each week but every one in seven years. In all of this we are called to be a part of a three-way relationship between God, people and planet. Interestingly, this relationship with the land is not about a respect for nature pointing back to a hunter-gatherer existence. It is clear from this passage and those that we read earlier, in Genesis, that farming is the way in which we are expected to interact with the natural world in our daily lives. We are called to roll our sleeves up and get involved. Biblically, it is OK to make adaptations of natural systems and to live off the fruits of creation, but it is not OK to farm beyond the limits of the land. We must leave the edges of our fields for the poor (Leviticus 19:9–10). The land must have its year of rest, when, presumably, wildlife will also take their share of its bounty (25:7).

If these guidelines are kept, there is a promise that the people will live in safety and have food to eat (v. 19). Clearly that is not the case today for the people of the Horn of Africa or those struggling after the Asian floods. Our collective loss of a sense of limits has led to our changing climate and many other environmental problems. Those suffering the consequences are often not those who have benefited from human overuse of the land.

Leviticus 25 provides a basis for a specific relationship to a specific land. Each tribe and family in Israel was given land as a gift from God, for themselves and for their descendants. If they fell into poverty and were forced to sell their land, their family could regain it in the year of jubilee. Today, many of the world's people live in cities, with global networks. We have lost the sense of connection to a specific location. We also need to regain our sense of relationship with our own land—be that rural or urban. In both situations, God gives us land as a gift, and nature as a blessing. He asks that we care for the land in which he places us, including the human elements, such as buildings, as well as the natural environment. Urban areas can seem less connected with nature, and yet it is often the natural elements, such as trees and lawns, that make them attractive.

5 Going beyond limits

Genesis 3:1–19

Borneo exports large amounts of tropical hardwood and has been clearing its forests for agriculture, especially the production of palm oil. In 2006, the carbon produced by the burning of its forest cover was greater than the whole of the UK carbon emissions that year from industry, transport and domestic use. Sadly, the soils exposed are quite thin and they depend on the rich tropical forest to replenish their nutrients. Without their natural forest cover, they provide a few short years of plenty but are rapidly exhausted. Many areas of former tropical forest are now degraded land with erosion on slopes. It is currently estimated that deforestation causes 20 per cent of all human greenhouse gas emissions. Ecologists warn that the logging of tropical forests worldwide is at an unsustainable level and we will soon reach 'peak timber', when we will no longer have forests to supply our current demand. This could cause financial collapse in countries whose economies have been built around timber export, in addition to the devastating effect on world biodiversity.

When we read the Genesis account of the fall of humanity, we usually see the taking of the forbidden fruit as an act of disobedience against God. It was disobedience that led to the expulsion from Eden. However, it is also significant to note that Eden's sin was greed.

Taking the forbidden fruit of Eden can be seen as a paradigm for the despoliation of the Amazon and Asian tropical forests. It parallels our disregard for the fragile ecology above the Alaskan oil reserves and our use of the earth's resources beyond its ability to regenerate. When will we learn the lesson of Eden? Possibly only when we experience the full consequences of our actions.

We should instead heed the practical words of Deuteronomy 20:19: 'When you lay siege to a city for a long time, fighting against it to capture it, do not destroy its trees by putting an axe to them, because you can eat their fruit. Do not cut them down. Are the trees of the field people, that you should besiege them?' This does not mean that it is acceptable for humans to go to war, but it does mean that nature should not be made the victim of human conflicts. We need to manage the resources of the planet for the good of all creatures.

6 The earth mourns

Hosea 4:1–3

Climate scientists predict an increase in floods and other extreme weather events as the planet warms through human-induced climate change. Jane Fucella is a friend of mine working with Interserve in Bangkok. Last year she wrote about the floods they had been experiencing:

One third of the country is under water. Eight million people are directly affected. Well over 500 are dead—either drowned, electrocuted, bitten by snakes, or dead through disease from floodwaters. Evacuation centres are full of people because the flood water is chest deep in their communities and houses. The water is black. Hundreds of crocodiles have escaped from farms and are on the loose. Those people who are still in their homes have no access to essential food and water. Sanitation is a disaster in flooded areas.

The words of Hosea seem strangely contemporary when read against such an account of devastation. Hosea saw a breakdown in the relationship between humans and God, which led to a breakdown in relationships among people and between humans and the rest of creation. Human injustice was rife and the inevitable result was bloodshed and pain.

An interesting phrase is found in verse 3: what does the writer mean by 'the land mourns'? The second half of the verse refers to the death of birds and fish. The biodiversity of the planet is adversely affected by our human conflicts and our consumerist greed. Once the relationships have broken down, human actions have no limitations and death and destruction are the inevitable consequences. This echoes the world described in Genesis 3, where we see that the land does not simply mourn but is cursed (3:17). There are different views on the nature of the fall. Many scholars see it in terms of relationship breakdown. Others go further and support the idea of a cosmic fall. In the latter view, nature has been fundamentally damaged, even though fallen creation continues to bear God's image and fallen humanity continues to radiate God's goodness and creativity. (We will explain this thinking further next week in a study of Romans 8:19–22.)

Guidelines

The Hebrew scriptures have much more to teach us about the natural world. We could look at the rest of the Pentateuch and find further guidelines for living within limits. Job is brought to awe and wonder considering the world that God has made, and his own concerns seem small compared with the workings of the universe. The prophets look forward to a world where peace, justice and fruitfulness have been restored. Isaiah 11 is especially famous, with its images of peace and harmony between the various creatures. Many of the Psalms tell of the wonder of God's creation, and Psalm 148 even speaks of creation worshipping God.

In all these passages, there is a sense of dependence on the relationships between God, people and planet. When humanity is reconciled with God, harmony in the other relationships follows. When humanity walks away from God, we find that human relationships are fraught and nature suffers. The overall theme is of a beautiful creation made by God, which has been damaged through careless treatment by humans.

We might think that the ideal future would be a return to the wild, living in amazing forests and mountain ranges. Although these environments are portrayed as precious to God, the future place shown for humans to inhabit is one that has been formed in interaction with humans. We are called to get involved with God's creation. Looking at our world today, this is a call not only to farm the land but also to take positive action to reduce climate change and restore the places that others have devastated. Our New Testament studies next week will take us further on this journey.

1 Born into his own creation

John 1:1–14

Most Christians will have particular memories of hearing this famous passage read. For many of us, it takes our thoughts to Christmas, when the focus is on the amazing truth that Jesus, the light of the world, was born among us—that God became human for our sake. So what has it got to do with ecology? The environmental focus of this passage comes from an understanding of how the doctrines of creation and incarnation interact. Jesus is revealed here in three unique ways: existing before the world began, being divine, and being the agent of creation. The passage reaches a climax in verse 14: 'the Word became flesh and made his dwelling among us'. The environmental implication of this statement is profound. When our holy and perfect Creator became a physical person, he affirmed the continuing goodness of his creation. In creating the universe, God brought light to the whole world. The darkness described in verse 5 is not part of God's good creation but is the very absence of that goodness. It is this darkness that has blinded human eyes, preventing people from recognising the light of Christ. Has it also led to their actions that have caused damage and destruction?

The logical conclusion is that when humanity embraces the light, it should also regain the Creator's love and care for his world. But what if the light has come purely to save humanity? This passage highlights the fact that humans can find full adoption as children of God through believing in Christ (vv. 12–13) and this gift is not offered to the rest of creation—but light is given to all. When God makes his dwelling among us, his glory shines through all creation. This idea picks up on a verse from Habakkuk: 'For the earth will be filled with the knowledge of the glory of the Lord, as the waters cover the sea' (2:14).

2 The miraculous catch of fish

John 21:1–14

During the 20th century, two world wars provided unintentional 'sabbath rests' for global fish populations. Today, fish such as cod and haddock are being fished beyond their capacity to replenish. If we keep fishing at unsustainable levels, we will eventually drive some species to extinction.

The story of the miraculous catch of fish is a glimpse of the abundance of restored creation through the resurrection of Christ. Like the birth of Christ, his bodily resurrection affirms God's creation and God's continuing purpose for it. If creation was simply a backdrop and God wished to redeem humans alone into a 'higher' spiritual realm, then we would expect Jesus to have been resurrected into a 'higher' non-physical form. This view might be attractive to those basing their views on Platonic thinking. In reality, though, Jesus rose in a new creation body that was physical: he could eat bread and fish; his disciples could touch him. The new creation we glimpse in the risen Christ is a very real physical realm that is wonderfully perfected and free from sin and death.

The miraculous catch of fish is a window on this new creation. In our world, we will always struggle. Harvests will fail us, both on land and in the sea, as a result of natural problems and because of our own overuse of the planet. On that post-resurrection morning in Galilee, Jesus revealed the abundance of a restored creation to his disciples with a catch that was beyond the resources of our present world.

At breakfast, Jesus blessed and broke bread for his disciples. Each time we break bread at Communion, we are reminded of the abundant life and hope found in the new creation. When we eat bread in our daily lives, we are also reminded that Christ makes ordinary things extraordinary. In Christ, physical and spiritual are intertwined in this world and the next. Thinking back to our world's fish stocks, we must examine our management of them. Do we think about sustainability when we buy fish? Do we encourage our politicians to follow sustainable policies? Through our actions, do we point to the resurrection or to death through overuse?

3 Creation groaning

Romans 8:18–25

I love autumn colour: for me, there is nothing better than walking in glorious golden woodland on a bright, crisp, sunny day. The colours are all a result of the breakdown of the leaves as they die away in preparation for the winter. So the wonderful colour, which seems so full of life, has death built into it.

Today we look at one of the classic passages used by those who seek a biblical approach to caring for the environment. Dropped into the middle of this famous chapter on faith is a significant statement about the state of creation and its future hope. We can imagine Paul pondering the natural world, with all its beauty but also with death and decay. The natural cycles of our world depend on death to sustain life, but this does not make it any less painful. Paul, in grappling with the suffering of this world, puts his hope in Christ and the future glory that Christ promises. Paul describes creation as groaning, bound in an endless cycle of decay. This bondage is not of its own making but is part of God's purpose in his plan for salvation—and there is good news: Christ has broken the power of sin and death through the cross so that creation can look toward a liberation from decay.

Suddenly we realise that the gospel is a whole lot bigger than we may have imagined. The power of the cross not only brings personal human redemption but also promises the end of death and pain for the whole of God's creation. Of course, we cannot interpret that promise within our own understanding of nature today: take away death and decay and we would soon have environmental collapse. The promise set before us is of a world transformed so that it can flourish in a completely new way.

The implications are enormous. If God has a redemption plan for the whole world, then the world cannot be seen simply as a stage on which the human drama of redemption is worked out. Nature is part of God's plan of redemption and our involvement in caring for the environment is therefore part of mission.

4 Held together in Christ

Colossians 1:15–23

For several years, I worked as a university chaplain. One of the things that I found interesting was the number of physics students who were Christians. As they studied the complexity of the universe and the perfection of the mathematics supporting it, they clearly found it but a short step to belief in a Creator God.

In this passage, Paul is explaining the cosmic nature of Christ to Christians in Colossae. He argues that Christ was the agent of creation in the past and has an ongoing role in sustaining creation in the present and future. Christ has made peace for all creation through his sacrifice on the cross. The perfection of cosmic mathematics points to a perfect Redeemer holding creation together and bringing it to harmony.

But there is also a major challenge for Christians. Christ is both chief (firstborn) over all creation and the head of the church, which is his body. As members of the church, we should point toward these cosmic truths in the way we live as Christians. We should work to bring peace to all creatures in God's world and to help nature and humanity find a restored relationship. This means that we need to think practically in the big and small decisions that we make in life. It is much easier to use disposable forks and plates for a church social, but does the waste produced point to a life-giving saviour? It may be quicker to drive to church than to walk, but, if you are fit and mobile, do you really need to? Then what about the church boiler? Our own church was unable to find a sustainable option to replace an ailing oil-fired one, but the search led members to think deeply about our faith. We are now searching out the most economic boiler possible and looking to technology to maximise efficiency. Many churches have found help through Eco-congregation, which provides a useful audit on the nuts and bolts of being the body of Christ in a creation-friendly way.

5 Creation made new

Revelation 21:1–5

Every so often, people come to me and say that there is no need to worry too much about caring for the earth because God promises to give us a completely new heaven and earth in the future. The word 'new' in Revelation 21:1, however, does not have that meaning. The Greek word is *kainos*, which means to be 'made new' or 'renewed'. It seems that God is into recycling. Far from being thrown into extinction like some cosmic paper plate, the new heaven and earth will be a redeemed and renewed form of our present heaven and earth.

It is impossible to know exactly what a renewed earth will look like. Revelation uses symbolic language to explain it further, saying that there will be no more 'sea' (v. 1). The sea is a symbol of chaos in Hebrew thought, and so its absence is symbolic of the end of the chaotic forces of evil. God dwells in the midst of his creation, and death and pain have been banished (v. 4). This passage echoes Isaiah 65:17 and the images there of a future harmony of creation. Whatever it looks like, it will be good!

The new creation is not just about the future, however. In the 2011 NIV translation of the Bible, 2 Corinthians 5:17 is rendered, 'Therefore, if anyone is in Christ, the new creation has come.' As the body of Christ, we demonstrate the new creation now and point to the future when all creation will be made new. How does that look in practice?

A Rocha is a Christian environmental charity that seeks to bring God's love to all creation. Its first project in the UK is called Living Waterways and is based in Southall, west London. In this intensely urban, inner-city area, Living Waterways is a parable of the glory that we hope for. When A Rocha started managing the project, it was an abandoned open space, marred by fly-tipping and covered in brambles. A Rocha worked to clean up the area to encourage wildlife and developed educational and leisure programmes to help local people connect with the natural world. Now, a rubbish-filled wasteland has become a haven for wildlife and a place for people to relax and enjoy the world of their Creator. Creation still groans in Southall, but Living Waterways points toward the hope of liberation.

6 Our gospel hope

Romans 5:1–5

What is Christian hope? In October 2011, a small group of theologians, environmental activists and scientists gathered to discuss the issue in the light of the current environmental crisis. The meeting was convened by the John Ray Initiative and A Rocha. The delegates were all 'opinion formers'—people whom others look to when trying to make sense of the environment from a Christian perspective.

The group identified three types of hope. The first is the hope that the problems can be solved: regarding climate change, this was a popular position ten years ago. We hoped that if the nations of the world all took action together, it would be possible to avert the worst effects of climate change. Ten years on, this hope looks distinctly thin. The second sort of hope is the eschatological hope, which we have already discussed in our study of Revelation 21. This gives a firm hope for a wonderful future, but we need to also interpret it in the present. As a group, we came to examine a third form of hope—that of living our Christian hope while experiencing severe difficulties in our present life. We called this 'robust hope'.

Our passage today gives a clear exposition of this robust Christian hope. It is based on our justification in Christ, which has restored our relationship with God. It looks to the future and the glory of God that will one day be revealed. It is not an otherworldly hope, however, but a tough reality that sustains us in the present. Paul speaks of a hope that comes out of suffering, that brings perseverance and strengthens character. The early church father Irenaeus believed that God uses suffering to strengthen Christians in their faith and life. Other Christians are wary of anything that might be seen to give a moral justification for suffering, but understand that suffering is a reality in our lives.

Christian hope is not dependent on easy circumstances, quick happy endings or health and prosperity. Most of us will struggle with personal sadness and pain during our lives. Our hope is that God is alongside us and that he works through our suffering. Our hope, shining through our weaknesses, points to the glory of the new creation, which is seen in each believer when we act out our resurrection hope in our daily lives.

Guidelines

This century is going to be tough. Climate change is already having major impacts around the world, which are going to become even more severe as the planet heats up. Combine this with the other problems outlined at the beginning of these studies and we realise that we are facing a difficult future. In our response, we need to think through the actions that could point to hope. As a church, we are in a unique position. Our international network of grassroots communities gives us insights into conditions in other parts of the world. We must keep these insights strong, to maintain support for some of the poorest in the world: there will be some in society who will want to pull up the drawbridge.

Locally we will also find ourselves in communities that are increasingly under pressure. As the oil supply begins to struggle to keep up with demand, everything will become much more expensive, from fuel to food. Our clothes and many goods in our daily lives are also made using oil or fossil fuel energy. How will we cope with very different circumstances in future? We have the spiritual resources to enable others to adjust to these difficulties, but we need to engage with our local communities to be able to use them. We have an amazing Christian hope. As we face a world in difficulties, each one of us is invited to respond to the challenge of making that hope visible to others.

• Our studies have shown that we hope for a renewed creation. Some people suggest that this means Christians need not worry about environmental care now. How would you respond to this argument?
• It is predicted that there will be 200 million environmental refugees by 2050. How will we speak up for these people and make sure that room is made for them in the rest of the world, including our own land?
• What do we need to do now to prepare our churches to be willing and able to support the poorer parts of the world, as things continue to get tougher toward the middle of the century?
• How can we best be examples of Christian hope to the people around us? What does this say about the way we might approach mission this century?

FURTHER READING

R. Bauckham, *Bible and Ecology*, DLT, 2010.

M.J. Hodson and M.R. Hodson, *Cherishing the Earth: how to care for God's creation*, Monarch Books, 2008.

M. Maslin, *Very Short Introduction to Global Warming*, OUP, 2004.

A Rocha (www.arocha.org) is an environmental mission working in conservation. It has projects in the UK and worldwide.

CRES (www.cres.org.uk) is a distance learning course combining Christian, rural and environmental studies.

Eco-congregation (www.ecocongregation.org) is a practical tool to use within your church.

The John Ray Initiative (www.jri.org.uk) combines science with environment and the Christian faith. The initiative is known for its conferences and courses and provides expert advice to other organisations.

Transition (www.transitionnetwork.org) is a secular network that works with communities to strengthen them at local level. Many Christians are involved.

Prayer in the New Testament

When we read through the New Testament, prayer can seem to be elusive: it's not always easy to find, particularly if we are looking for specific prayers or ways in which to pray. Reading between the lines, though, we can see that prayer lies at the foundation of the writings of the New Testament, and all those who are called to follow the Way are expected to pray. It is perhaps surprising, then, but reassuring, that even the first disciples were confused about how to pray and what to say: they asked Jesus, who gave them the words that form the Lord's Prayer today (Matthew 6:9–13; Luke 11:2–4).

The Lord's Prayer only receives a brief mention over the coming two weeks. Instead, some of the other more recognisable New Testament prayers will be considered, along with a few unexpected passages. The prayer we discover within the New Testament reveals the importance of corporate prayer and prayer for others, as well as time in quiet personal prayer. Our private and personal prayer should be important in our faith life and relationship with God: out of it comes our intercessory prayer and prayer offered together with others, whether in church, in a home group or in a prayer group.

As our lives become busier, it is often our time in prayer that dwindles away, sometimes without our realising it. For those of us who serve within the church in an ordained or lay role, keeping prayer alive can be difficult, as it can be for those whose life is filled with work and family responsibilities. Over the next two weeks we shall look at some of the prayer to be found in the New Testament that may help us reflect upon the prayer within our own lives. On some days, there will be suggestions for ways in which to pray with the Bible passage—suggestions that can be used alone or with others. If using the prayer with others, anything shared and spoken needs to be held in confidence, acceptance and love.

How can the prayer of the New Testament help us, or show us the way, to deeper prayer and encounter with God?

All Bible quotations are taken from the New Revised Standard Version.

1 Quietness

Today's passage reveals the deep need of Jesus to be alone with God. Rising early, he goes off to a quiet place where he can bring to God his personal thoughts and feelings, concerns and anxieties. In the quietness, too, there is the opportunity to listen with a deeper attentiveness to anything that God might communicate to him within his heart. If Jesus needed this time away in quietness, how much more do we?

So, in the quietness of his prayer and solitude, Jesus not only brings his thoughts to God but is able to listen to the movement of God within, to discern what he is to do. He is able to seek guidance and clarity, before the other disciples find him and want to know what is to happen next (v. 37). He is therefore very clear about the direction they are to take together and the unfolding of his ministry of bringing God's love to all (v. 38).

Yet neither the Gospel nor the epistles tell us exactly what we are to do in the quietness of prayer. There are clues about how to formulate intercessory prayers, and Paul tells us to 'pray without ceasing' (1 Thessalonians 5:17), yet there is nothing about contemplative prayer in the quietness. This is where we need to read between the lines, and maybe refer to the writings of those who have sought out silent prayer—for example, the Desert Fathers and Mothers, and authors such as Thomas Merton and Esther de Waal.

It's interesting to note that it is only Jesus, and not his disciples, who is recorded in the Gospels as having times of quiet prayer. Does this mean that quiet prayer is only for those in 'top' leadership roles in the church? Obviously not, but each of us needs to discover how quietness with God can be part of our prayer life. Not everyone will find it comfortable, especially as our world is full of noise. It may be that, like Jesus, to be quiet with God, we need to find a place that is away from our own home. Within our own home and church, it isn't always easy to be still and quiet with God in prayer.

If you have a particular role to play in church, how does that affect, influence or shape the way you pray and the time you spend in quietness?

2 Perseverance

Luke 11:5–13

There is the saying that practice makes perfect. Some of the things that we learn to do only take a little practice, while other things take a great deal of practice, and perseverance is needed if we are to get even a small way towards being perfect. Seeking perfection, though, can place upon us a great deal of stress. Moving to the Church in Wales has meant my learning to speak and read Welsh, so I have needed much perseverance in seeking an 'OK' standard rather than an unrealistic 'perfect'! This relates to prayer as well. We do not need to be perfect—whatever 'perfection' means—but prayer does require practice and perseverance, as well as the desire and willingness to be our own self in our prayer and before God. Paul, writing to the Romans, offers a little reassurance that when we do not know how to pray, the Spirit will interpret our sighs and inner confusion (Romans 8:26).

In today's Bible passage, the disciples have asked Jesus how to pray and, having given them the Lord's Prayer, Jesus continues with a parable about perseverance and persistence. He says that although our friends or neighbours may not always have time for us, God is like the one who opens the door in the darkness and gives what is asked of him, whatever we need. God is always ready to hear our prayer: he is the unsleeping God (see Psalm 121:4). However often we bring the same requests to God, it remains important that we do not stop, but continue; no prayer is a waste of time or goes unheard.

To ask is to express our deepest concerns and needs in prayer. To search is to seek the way of prayer that is right for us and for the kind of prayer being offered. As we come to pray, we discover the door opened to us through which we can 'be' with God.

Ignatian spirituality teaches us to ask for a grace, or a gift of the Spirit, as we begin our time in prayer. Our request may be for perseverance as we pray, or for inner peace, God's love, compassion, hope, or to feel the touch of the Spirit. What is the grace of God that you would ask for as you begin to pray today?

3 Wonder

1 Corinthians 13

This is a familiar passage, and it is not a prayer in itself. Nevertheless, we can read it prayerfully, allowing it to reveal the movement of our spiritual journey from the beginning of our faith to the present. It reveals, too, the need to pause and reflect on how our prayer has changed and evolved over the years through a growing relationship held in the love of God.

We see here, albeit dimly, something of the love and wonder of God. Paul speaks of how we see as children and how we see with maturity (and how we will see even more clearly when we come face to face with God). The way we make conversation and relate to others changes as we move from childhood to teenage years, and then into adulthood. Has the same happened in the way we speak to God in prayer?

The prayer we offered as a child, or at the beginning of our journey of faith, will deepen and develop into a more mature conversation as our understanding of God grows. Paradoxically, though, as we grow in faith, commitment and discipleship, the prayers we offer—communally and privately—may increasingly acknowledge that we can only know God 'dimly' (v. 12). Yet we also recognise that, through God's love, all that we do not know or understand now will become clear when we encounter God face to face.

The love offered by God is a sustaining love, a patient love. It is a love that takes us, and our prayer, exactly as we are. It gives us the freedom truly to wonder, in awe, that we are not only loved but called to come to God in prayer. Wonder has been described as the forgotten element in the spiritual life, perhaps especially in adults. Yet, to wonder, child-like, can help us see beyond ourselves to the transforming love of God. What does it mean to you to 'wonder'? What does it mean to be loved by God?

How has your prayer journey developed? On a piece of paper, write out a prayer map that marks the 'high and low' moments of transformation—for example, special times of knowing God's presence with you, having a sense of God's calling, or committing to a deeper involvement in the life of the church, as well as times of questioning, despair, doubt and the feeling that God is very distant. Include anything that seems important, and then pray about any insights you receive.

4 Humility

Once we begin to sense something of the wonder of God's love within the framework of a deepening faith, along with it arrives the awareness of the need to 'walk humbly with your God' (Micah 6:8).

To be humble is not to belittle ourselves but, rather, to respect ourselves as we seek also to show respect to others. It does not mean playing down our own giftedness or ignoring the importance of praising another's service or contribution. To be humble is to come to the ground of our being. It is to accept that we will never reach 100 per cent perfection but should strive to do our best. To be humble is to be aware of our shortcomings and our need for forgiveness.

To pray is to come to the heart and centre of who we are, encountering God in the place where, in humility, only the truth can be spoken. In that place, the truth is revealed, and in that place, God is present. The parable of the Pharisee and the tax collector shows that we often require only a few words to express a prayer from the heart.

The tax collector reaches deep within, to the place of inner truthfulness, and offers a prayer of genuine humility and need. The Pharisee, by contrast, offers a prayer about his own self-worth and goodness, fuelled by contempt for the tax collector.

The tax collector prays in contrition for sins committed, whether actual or assumed, and from his words comes the Jesus Prayer ('Lord Jesus Christ, Son of God, have mercy on me, a sinner')—a prayer that is both simple and extremely profound. Whatever our role within the life of the church, this is an essential prayer for all who follow the path of faith. It is a prayer that we can pray alone, and yet it unites us as one. It grounds us equally in companionship as disciples, and reminds us of the support we need from one another as we seek the way of humility.

It is not always easy to reach a true understanding of what humility means within our daily life. To pray this prayer will enable us not only to know ourselves better but also to become more empathetic and understanding of the people around us.

5 Thanksgiving

Romans 1:7–15

From the depths of humility we move to the heights of thanksgiving. The prayer Paul writes at the beginning of this letter thanks God for the faith of the people of the Roman church. He thanks them for giving him assistance as he has assisted them, encouraging them in this mutual support for the way ahead. Paul also lets them know that even when facing adversity, he will offer his ministry to them. Paul is speaking of himself but, unlike the Pharisee in yesterday's reading, his focus is totally upon God and the sacrifice of Christ for all.

This is a prayer of thanksgiving and intercession, yet it has the feel of a general report, including an account of how Paul is and what he's doing. Paul sets prayer at the heart of the discipleship upon which the rest of the epistle is based, and flows easily from the genre of prayer to that of a letter (as he does in other epistles).

This may be a familiar style of prayer to you: perhaps you too would write a letter to a friend in which prayer and news are interwoven, sharing information and bringing it to God at the same time. It may also be a style of prayer that is offered to open a meeting or gathering, flowing naturally into the business of the meeting.

Many of Paul's prayers in the New Testament consist of thanksgiving. It's easy to forget to include thanksgiving when we pray, encompassing not only our own joy in faith and ministry but also joy in the ministry offered by others. We may find that it feels a little uncomfortable to give thanks for everything we do. This can be a way of discerning our priorities or direction in ministry, deciding whether we are doing too much or not enough, and seeking God's ongoing support of all that we are offering.

How often do you pray a prayer of thanksgiving, for yourself and for others? Is it a natural part of your prayer life, or does it feel uncomfortable to pray for all you offer?

Perhaps you would like to read through these verses of prayer and report again, and then rewrite them, following their sequence and structure, so the words relate to your situation and needs or those of someone you know.

6 Rejoicing

Philippians 4:4–9

Philippi, already an ancient city at the time Paul visited, was situated on the overland route that connected Rome to the east. It was inhabited mainly by Romans but also by some Greeks and Jews. Paul had the challenge of speaking the gospel message to a largely Gentile population there. He needed to speak to them in a language they understood, carefully unfolding the dramatic story of Jesus in a way that would catch their imaginations. More importantly, he needed to speak with words that conveyed the truth and the depth of meaning that lay behind the gospel.

The people heard his message and a church was founded (see Acts 16). In this letter, Paul rejoices with them for their ongoing journey of faith. He reminds them not to have their heads turned away from God by the life of others in the city—to take care and not be led astray. Throughout the letter, though, there is a sense of joy.

This is a joy that embraces the ups and downs of life, a joy that comes from knowing God. It is far more than an emotion felt: it is more like a way of being. Joy means having a sense of contentment, but not complacency, in the knowledge that we rest and live in God's love. For Paul, to know this inner joy meant that prayer was essential—for maintaining peace of mind as well as deepening the relationship with God.

Again, these verses are not written by Paul as a specific prayer, but they are prayerful words placed within a chapter of his letter. They are words that offer encouragement to others to bring all commendable things to God in prayer. Importantly, they encourage us to rejoice. Our prayer need not always be solemn and serious, full of our deep concerns and worries. At times it needs to be upbeat and fun, full of the joy and laughter of life, expressed with rejoicing from our hearts. There is a place for both approaches: in his letter, Paul exhorts us to rejoice and, through making our requests known to God, to find a peace that passes all understanding.

Is there a place for joy and laughter in your prayer? What does joy mean to you? What does the peace of God mean to you?

Guidelines

The best-known prayer from the New Testament is probably the all-encompassing Lord's Prayer. The disciples, wanting to know how to pray, did as we ourselves might have done at times in our spiritual journey: they asked the person they thought would know best how to help them. The prayer below is my rewriting of the prayer that Jesus taught the disciples.

Holy and eternal God,
your name is precious
May heaven and earth be as one,
held in love and peace.
May all our daily needs be met.
In our straying and wrongdoing,
pour upon us your forgiveness,
and enlarge our hearts to bring forgiveness
to those who cause us pain and hurt.
Lead us always to walk in the light of your love
and away from all that tempts us.
For you are the God of all creation,
throughout this and every age. Amen

1 Prayer for the readers

Ephesians 3:14–21

The letter to the Ephesians is one of encouragement and support to those who follow the way of Christ, reminding those who hear or read it of the gifts and blessings that God has poured upon them through the Spirit. In places, Paul points out the dangers of straying back into their old way of life (for example, 4:17; 5:8) and tells them to be prepared and equipped with the whole armour of God to withstand the temptations of the world (6:10–17). Overall, though, it seems to be a letter written in gentleness and peace, embracing the Ephesian church in prayer. Paul is concerned for the general and spiritual well-being of the people, so he prays for them and encourages them to pray for him too (6:19), that he may continue to preach the word of God boldly.

The prayer in today's passage holds within it all that is necessary for us as we walk the Christian path. We may use these words as a prayer for ourselves on our personal journey with God, or as a prayer for others. As Paul asked the people of Ephesus to pray for him, the words may also be prayed for those who lead the church today, asking that they may be sustained, renewed and enabled through the Spirit for the ministry they offer.

Often, congregation members will ask their priest, minister or church leader to pray for them, but how often does the church leader ask the rest of the congregation to pray for him or her? To ask for prayer is not a sign of weakness or lack of faith; rather, it exhibits a belief in the power of prayer and, at times, a need to hear someone else put into words an appropriate prayer that the one asking perhaps cannot offer for themselves.

Read through the prayer in these verses, slowly, as it is written. Then think of someone known to you—for example, your church leader, someone just beginning the Christian journey or someone taking on a new role in church. Then read the prayer again and include the name of that person in verses 16–19. In a group setting, each person could pray a different name, thus making it a prayer for a wider community.

2 Healing and honesty

Mark 10:46–52

The passage is not a prayer, but, when we uncover the layers of the story, it reveals many elements that are important components of our prayer and relationship with God, such as taking a risk, being open and vulnerable, being honest, and having the courage to speak. In the restoration of sight to Bartimaeus, there is a question that needs to be answered honestly before Jesus brings healing. Jesus asks, 'What do you want me to do for you?' to which Bartimaeus replies, 'Let me see again.'

It is a very simple question and a very simple answer. Or is it? It is a potentially life-changing question and a risk-taking answer. Healed and able to see, Bartimaeus enters a new chapter of his life. His old life has gone and he walks into a newly transformed world where he can see, where he is accepted as the person he is, rather than being sidelined, ignored and treated as an outcast, begging on the roadside.

It took courage to be transformed in this way, and it took honesty to say what he really wanted. Nothing would ever be the same for him, and there was no guarantee of how secure his life would be without the meagre income that he gained from begging. He took the risk, knowing and believing that Jesus could heal him, and trusting that all would be well for him afterwards.

Reading this passage challenges us to 'see' our own blind spots—for example, our own personal fears, anxieties and prejudices, which may make us blind to the needs of others around us. It challenges us to have the courage to be honest in bringing to God what is really important to us. Bartimaeus shows how we may pray with conviction and be willing to stand out in a hostile world, to give voice to our own areas of vulnerability and need. He makes us aware that the replies we give to God can change our lives and set us along a different path in faith, recognising all that needs changing and healing in our lives.

This passage can also be used in a wider context, to give us eyes to discern with honesty God's call to the local church. It encourages us to seek out the areas in need of healing or renewal, and the courage to step out in faith.

3 Prayer of transformation

Romans 12:1–8

Freed from the constrictions placed upon him by the 'world', Bartimaeus was able to present his body 'as a living sacrifice, holy and acceptable to God' (v. 1). Once healed, he was no longer prohibited from worshipping in the synagogue. Thankfully, today, we can all come to God in prayer and worship, privately and publicly, regardless of the physical healing our bodies may need. Transformation comes through knowing God, and knowing that God accepts and welcomes us as we are.

To transform our minds, we need to listen to God in the quietness of prayer, and to the people who know us well. Listening to God with care can take us deeper within, to discover more of our selves and of the parts of us that still need transformation. Listening to others and hearing their stories can help us to look at our own journey, accepting, celebrating and rejoicing in the similarities and differences—as we will all experience the transforming presence of God in different ways.

Today's passage describes how we are to live as Christians to whom God has reached out in love with the power to transform us into the likeness of Christ. That transformation draws us closer to God, so that we may 'discern what is the will of God' and all that is acceptable, good and perfect (v. 2). To be transformed by God is not to have the essence of our selves changed, but to begin to know our selves more as we are known by God. It is to have the whole of our being brought into unity, a unity that includes and highlights our strengths and gifts while acknowledging our weaknesses and limitations. Being transformed by God's love also reveals the gifts with which we have been blessed—gifts that we can offer in faith and service (v. 6).

What does the word 'transformation' mean to you within the context of this passage? How much have you learnt about faith and prayer by listening to other people's stories about their walk with God? How easy is it to share something of your own experience of being transformed by God?

4 Prayer for others (1)

Today and tomorrow we reflect upon the high priestly prayer of Jesus. It is a prayer of intercession, and in today's passage the intercession is for the first disciples. Jesus prays for them, knowing that they will soon be left without his physical presence to guide and support them. He calls upon God to watch over them, protect them and sanctify them in and with the truth—truth that will soon be made visible through the ministry they offer. Jesus prays specifically for the disciples and for no one else, as he knows that his own time on earth will shortly come to an end. He lifts them to God in prayer, asking that they might continue to be held in love as they begin a new and unknown chapter in their lives.

Jesus has washed their feet and has broken bread and poured out wine to unite his disciples in anticipation of the church that they will build up in his name. The journey that lies ahead will not be an easy one for the disciples, so a mutual bond of love and support will be necessary as they struggle to preach God's word to an uncomprehending world. As they come closer to sharing in the ministry entrusted to them, Jesus holds them in prayer.

In the church of today, every person has a part to play, as the church cannot survive with only one, or a few, doing everything. There needs to be prayer for the encouragement, support and enabling of all who are disciples of Jesus today. We need to ask God to watch over those who engage with the life of church in any way, to be with them and protect them from all that may bring a sense of disillusionment. Prayer is needed that the church might be a place of welcome, beginning with a drawing together of the whole congregation into a unity of prayerful discipleship, in faith and through the sharing of the bread and wine of Communion.

Who in your congregation is in need of your intercession for the ministry they offer? Which group or person may be struggling to bring a new venture or area of ministry to birth?

5 Prayer for others (2)

John 17:20–26

In the remaining verses of Jesus' prayer in John 17, the focus moves from the disciples to the rest of the world. Jesus looks beyond the local mission and needs of his first disciples to the wider implications of life being lived out in the world—a world that is often hostile rather than welcoming. This world is in need of love, peace and a hope of unity, rather than the disintegration of unity that is fuelled by the unwillingness to accept and rejoice in all that each person can offer. Yet those who seek to share the good news of God find a very mixed reception in the world: Jesus' prayer therefore remains relevant for us today.

Jesus prays that the people of the world may hear the word of God being spoken to them. These people could include those who refuse to hear, those who have not yet heard and those who, for whatever reason, cannot hear. We rarely get to know the effect that our spoken words have on the people who hear them, whether through general conversation, a sermon or a passing comment. Generalised words may touch a place of need or concern in the one who hears them within the specific context of their life at that present moment. Our words can, like a pebble thrown into the water, send out far-reaching ripples, bringing about a response that we would never expect and will probably never hear about.

The prayer that Jesus prays is for the world and for the contacts that his disciples will have with the world. It is a prayer that Jesus prays for us, too, as disciples living the Christian life today, asking God to be with us as we seek to draw others to hear his word.

Our prayers of intercession naturally include the needs of our local communities and the global world community. They might include, too, those who work within the world, especially those who face difficulties or prejudice because of the faith they proclaim. Jesus' prayer of intercession embraces all who are a part of the life and mission of the church.

How is the prayer of intercession offered in your church? How do you pray for those who live out their faith in the wider world? What are your prayers for the church in the life of your local community?

6 The water of life

Revelation 22

We come today to the last chapter of Revelation. It opens with a description of the city of God, where the fruit trees bring healing, where God is the light of the world, and where the river holding the water of life flows from the throne of the Lamb. There is enough imagery within those opening verses to inspire many a prayer, in word, in imagination and in the creativity of artwork both drawn and written. Through it all runs the call of God to come, to worship and to be all that we have been created to be.

There is also the call to live a holy and pure life. John writes that those who have 'washed their robes' are blessed (v. 14). The washing of robes was associated with entry into the holy city, where clothes had to be clean and unsoiled—a metaphor for the life lived in faithfulness to God—so the call to 'come' to the heavenly city depended upon having lived a pure life. The last verse, thankfully, is one of benediction, as it is only through the grace of God that we will ever have a chance to be washed clean by forgiveness and so come to the water of life in the heavenly city.

Prayer could be described as our spiritual water of life, a life force that flows through us as we seek to hear God's call. How is God's call 'to come' heard in the church and by us personally? What does it mean to come to God in faith and discipleship? In our prayers, these questions play a part as we discern more deeply what it really means to us to be a Christian in the world of today. How we respond to these questions will also depend upon how we 'see' or image God. The questions could be discussed at a group meeting looking at prayer and God's call, and will reveal many answers.

The call 'to come' is also a call to participate actively in service through our particular giftedness. It might involve seeing a gift in someone else, and then enabling and encouraging them to be aware of that gift and to offer it for the benefit of others. Who has helped and enabled you to discover your giftedness?

How do you come to God in prayer, and how might you do it differently, having read these notes over the last fortnight?

Guidelines

The New Testament authors reveal that prayer is at the heart of all they have written—prayer for themselves and for others. This prayer was written to be prayed individually but can also be used within a group:

O God, you have spoken through the prophets of old, and you have spoken through your Son. Open my ears to your prayer for me. Open my heart to the prayer I am to offer for others. Open my eyes to see the prayer I am to pray for the world. Open my lips to speak in love and hope for my own journey in faith, and for others travelling the same pathway. Open my whole self to be transformed by your love, that in thanksgiving and rejoicing I may, with your help, follow and serve you as you have called me.

FURTHER READING

Oscar Cullman, *Prayer in the New Testament*, SCM, 1995.
Peter Hannon SJ, *The Quiet Revolution*, Columba, 2010.
Jean Vanier, *Drawn into the Mystery of Jesus through the Gospel of John*, DLT, 2004.

Passiontide and Easter

Sin, solidarity and love: these are the profound themes of the next two weeks. The fifth week of Lent and Holy Week are known collectively as Passiontide—derived from the Latin word for 'suffering'—when Christians meditate especially on the suffering and death of Jesus and what they mean for us. During the next two weeks, we will use the readings set for the Eucharist each day by the Church of England and the Roman Catholic Church, chosen by those churches to help us enter more deeply into the Church's most holy season.

The Bible was compiled, in part, by the Christian Church, so it is fitting that we read it in common with the Church too. We will gain additional strength from knowing that we are not praying and reflecting alone but that these passages and themes are ones that our fellow believers are subjecting to equally intense appreciation during this fortnight, which is central to the faith.

Unless otherwise stated, quotations are from the Jerusalem Bible.

1 All equal before God

John 8:1–11

I can still remember putting little stones in the lock of the caretaker's door at school. I'm not quite sure why I did this, but I do remember my friends egging me on. Yet when the caretaker arrived and wanted to know who was responsible, all the fingers pointed at me, from the same hands that had enthusiastically passed me pebbles for my nefarious work a few minutes before. Needless to say, I alone spent the remainder of the lunch hour with the caretaker's screwdriver, taking off the lock and removing the offending items.

Many of us will remember situations when we've done something wrong and all fingers point at us. It's a horrid feeling when the pang felt by our conscience is exacerbated by the accusations from people who are no better than we are or even encouraged us in what we've been doing.

The Gospel reading of the woman caught in adultery is, therefore, a very fitting beginning to our Passion reflections, because Jesus uses it to place everyone at the same level: we are all sinners in need of forgiveness. If there is one of you who has not sinned, he says, then by all means throw the first stone, point the first finger. He knows, however, that there is no one in that situation. No matter how good or bad a Lent we've had, whether our resolutions and penances have been kept or we've strayed, we come to these two weeks all in the same boat—one that's sinking and needs help.

It's also important to notice how Jesus handles the situation. He is silent for most of it, occupied with drawing on the ground. He is the last to say anything to the woman about her sin, showing more interest in the fact that his words have had the desired effect, causing even the elders to go away. It seems that the casting of stones, the public humiliation and the desire to scapegoat another and claim the moral high ground are all worse sins in the Lord's eyes than adultery. 'Don't do that,' says Jesus clearly to the woman, but the point of the story is clearly to emphasise not her failings but those of the people who would accuse her. At the beginning of Passiontide, our egos are brought back down to earth.

2 God's imaginative solution

Numbers 21:4–9

We have short memories. I so easily forget all the goodness of God to me, and the ways in which prayer has been answered and I have been protected and cared for and carried through the storm. Instead, I look only at the present moment or think about what terrible things might happen in the future, and want to know why God isn't solving all the problems now. In today's passage, the Israelites, whom God has rescued from slavery in Egypt and fed with manna from heaven, are full of complaints about where they now are and what they have to eat. The very thing that previously saved them from starvation (see Numbers 11) they judge to be unworthy of them, now that their lot has improved—and all of a sudden, snakes come among them and attack them.

God, whose imagination and capacity to save we so often doubt, takes the situation and reverses it: the Israelites hate the very thing that once saved them (the manna), so God takes something else that they now find hateful (the snakes) and makes it a means of their being saved. Moses fashions a bronze snake and places it on a standard, and those who behold it are preserved from death. Jesus' Passion, too, will take that which we hate and which destroys us—death—and make it the means by which we are saved.

In the Gospels, Jesus often said to those who listened to him that if they had read their scriptures properly, they would have recognised and believed in him (see Matthew 12:3–8; 21:42–44; John 5:39–40). The taking of an instrument of hate and making it an instrument of love (which finds its supreme example in the cross) is no new thing: here in the wilderness, God uses what his people fear, to give them hope and new life. This does not stop with the cross, either: we are invited to find God and his saving work precisely in those things which, in our lives, seem only to deal death.

3 Slavery to sin

John 8:31–38

Addictions seem to grow in number: in the old days, you were addicted to tobacco, booze or drugs, but now there's sex, gambling, the internet, shopping and probably many more things that I've not even thought of. There is a danger, though, that we think we can restrict 'addiction' to certain particular things. Human beings are addictive creatures generally: our entire lives are based on patterns, and we get into habits and practices and tend to do things in routines and rituals. Most of us shower or shave or dress in the same way each morning, for example. Without these good habits, life would be impossible: just imagine having to invent a new way to dress every day! Yet not only can these good habits turn into compulsions and obsessions but there are plain bad addictions and patterns as well, which damage us even more straightforwardly.

Sin, being the basic messed-up nature of humanity, is at the heart of this problem. Sinful patterns of behaviour are addictive: they are habits in which we get tied up. It is Jesus' dealing with this negative addiction that we are considering during these two weeks. How are we freed from our bad habits, our addiction to sin?

In the Jerusalem Bible, Jesus puts it like this: 'If you make my word your home you will indeed be my disciples; you will learn the truth and the truth will make you free' (vv. 31–32). Just as we get into bad habits by doing the same actions again and again and making them part of who we are, so Jesus invites us to make him part of who we are: 'make my word your home', or, more precisely, make yourself part of him. This means finding a new way of living. Just like a bad habit, the good habit takes time to establish: we become his disciples and we learn the truth, which are things that take time and patience. The Lord assures us, though, that if we abide in him and learn from him, then this new way of living, these new habits, will make us free.

4 Dead and buried?

John 8:51–59

Living in time—as we do, being people who are born and who die—we have an understandable tendency to think of absolutely everything in the same terms. The people of Israel to whom Jesus addressed himself were clearly no different from us. So crazy was his talk about not seeing death, and about the dead Abraham rejoicing to see his day, that people assumed he was mad. They even wanted to stone him, so upsetting was this kind of talk to their understanding of life.

We can even see our own faith in the same way, if we think of Jesus as a man who lived and died and rose again a long time ago, whose memory we gather in church to recall and be inspired by. Yet this is to minimise our faith and Jesus himself. Jesus is not just human. Christians know him to be fully human and fully divine, and so, as the Son of God, the second person of the Trinity, he has always been and will always be: there was never a time when he wasn't. He is as alive today as he was 2000 years ago; in fact, thanks to his ascension, which allows his Spirit to be in all places at all times, he is more present with us now than when he walked the earth in flesh, even if it sometimes doesn't seem so. We should not forget that plenty of people did not believe or listen to him then, never mind now.

In Jesus, the beginning and the end (as he describes himself in Revelation 22:13), the past becomes present. That is how he could say, 'Your father Abraham rejoiced to think that he would see my Day; he saw it and was glad' (v. 56) of a person who had died thousands of years before. As we approach the time of Jesus' Passion, therefore, we do not just have to make an effort of imagination to think what it must have been like. Jesus, by his Spirit, is with us now and will guide and direct our prayers, so that as we journey through this season we can truly experience something of the death and resurrection of God incarnate.

5 It takes time

John 10:31–42

Fr Christopher Jamison, the former Abbot of Worth, made famous by the BBC TV programme *The Monastery*, when asked why he became a monk, said that the reason he joined the monastery was not the same as the reason why he stayed. He found that he had changed over time and been led deeper into the mystery of God and the mystery of himself.

Those listening to Jesus are about to stone him for blasphemy: they cannot understand that he is both God and man. In our previous reading, Jesus made a statement expressly claiming divinity when he echoed the words of God to Moses, saying to his interlocutors, 'Before Abraham was, I am' (John 8:58; see Exodus 3:14). They attempted to stone him then, too.

Although, in Western culture, Christians may not be stoned today for believing Jesus to be the Son of God, people are still somewhat incredulous, and even those who have started coming to church often find the claim hard to understand or accept. Yet, we need time to journey in our faith; rarely are we given a bolt from the blue. Jesus recognises this need in the people to whom he is speaking in Jerusalem: 'Even if you refuse to believe in me, at least believe in the work I do' (v. 38). There is nowhere too far back to start in our faith. We can do this trustfully, for Jesus' Spirit draws us on—and we will not just stop there. If our hearts are open, he will lead us from belief just in the external works (wonderful though they are) to a living sense of Jesus as human and divine. As Jesus says, straight after urging his listeners to believe his works, 'Then you will know for sure that the Father is in me and I am in the Father' (v. 38). If we are not sure what to believe and are overwhelmed, especially in this season of the Christian year, we need not worry. As we simply participate in prayer and worship, God will draw us into that life of Father, Son and Spirit in his own good time.

6 Good and bad?

John 11:45–56

Very rarely in this world do we have a morally unambiguous choice. We often have to choose the lesser of two evils—or, at least, there will be some negative consequences to making the right decision, even when it clearly is the right decision to make. It is easy for us, if we love films where there's a 'good guy' and a 'bad guy', to see the Bible in a similar light. This is even more true when we are thinking about Jesus, who was an unambiguous good guy: those with whom he disagrees or comes into conflict must, we think, be simply and straightforwardly 'bad'.

In Passiontide, the Pharisees and the Jewish religious authorities (especially the high priest) are very easy to paint in this simplistic fashion. Yet here they have a genuine dilemma. If they stop Jesus, they will be silencing someone who, they admit, is 'working all these signs' (v. 47); but if they do not stop him, such a tumult may result that the occupying Roman authorities (who enforced law and order by the most brutal methods) will come and destroy the temple. This would not be like someone coming and knocking down our parish church, horrid though that would be. The temple held the Holy of Holies, the place where God's presence dwelt—the centre of the faith of Israel. Without the temple, it was almost impossible for there to be true religion. (This is why the Israelites ask, 'How could we sing the Lord's song in a foreign land?' in Psalm 137:4, NRSV.) If someone is threatening all that you hold most dear, their death can suddenly seem far less alarming and unthinkable than it would under more ordinary circumstances.

One of the tasks of this time of year is not just to read and reflect on the goodness and sufferings of our Saviour, but to enter sympathetically into the minds of those who killed him. The same crowds who cried 'Hosanna!' on Palm Sunday would later cry 'Crucify!' Until we can see that this is exactly how well-meaning souls like us behave, we won't have understood the Passion in any depth; nor will we have understood ourselves.

Guidelines

This week leading up to Holy Week has been a time of scene-setting. We've reflected on our equality before God, our addiction to sin and the fact that we share in the events surrounding the Lord at that first Passiontide 2000 years ago—both by the power of his Spirit and because we are capable of exactly the same actions when everything that we hold dear is under assault. Yet we've also seen how growing in our understanding and faith takes time, and how God knows and anticipates this; so we need not feel pressured but can let the events that are about to unfold wash over and affect us as they will. There's no hurry to get to the end, at this instant.

We have also seen that God's love is incredibly imaginative: he uses the very means of death to be means of life and glory. This is about to be made amazingly clear in the coming seven days, when we run the gamut of emotions from the triumph of Palm Sunday (perhaps you celebrated this in church today before you read *Guidelines*?) through the agony of Good Friday and the waiting of Holy Saturday to the unsurpassed glory of Easter Day.

1 The lavishness of God

John 12:1–11

A characteristic we often see in those who have cottoned on to Jesus' identity is generosity. Zacchaeus the tax collector not only gives away half of his possessions but also promises to repay four times as much to those he's defrauded (Luke 19:8); others go praising God and are unable to stop telling everyone what has happened (Luke 18:42; Mark 1:45); now Mary, whose brother Lazarus was raised from the dead by Jesus, comes and pours out 300 denarii worth of ointment on her Lord's feet.

We tend to believe, perhaps especially in Britain, that moderation is a virtue: we expect behaviour to be fair and reasonable. In some spheres this might be sensible, but it has little to say to us as Christians in Holy Week. We are walking a journey that leads to God incarnate dying for love of each one of us and then being raised from the dead. There is nothing moderate, fair or reasonable about that. God is irrationally and irresponsibly in love with us and will hold nothing back to win us to himself again. The problem is that we don't really believe it. How could I be that worthwhile? I know myself only too well, or so I think. Yet Mary's amazing gesture demonstrates that God knows us even better, and that taking his love for us to heart produces the same uncalculating, irresponsible response to God and his world. We need more real religious extremism—extreme love, extreme forgiveness, extreme generosity, extreme prayer.

Judas, who has not understood what Jesus is all about, gives the apparently moral, responsible response: Mary's money is being wasted and could have been spent on the poor. One denarius was a day's wage, so this is almost a year's salary that has been poured out. Yet the poor were not poor because of Mary's extravagance, any more than the poor are poor today because a church spends money on a stained-glass window or a silver chalice for Holy Communion. God does not want us to skimp on one thing so that we can spend on another; he wants us to be lavish about everything, for he is lavish in his love of us. Mary has just anointed the feet of the Son of God; the Son of God, on Maundy Thursday, will wash the feet of his disciples, giving abundant love in return for love.

2 Being where Jesus is

John 13:21–30

What is at the heart of our Holy Week experience? It is being with Jesus, retracing and reliving the last days of his life, that we may share with him even more powerfully in his resurrection. John's Gospel is a wonderful help to us in this because, in many ways, it focuses on being where Jesus is. At the beginning of his Gospel, John records, 'No one has ever seen God. It is God the only Son, who is close to the Father's heart, who has made him known' (1:18). The Greek word *kolpon*, translated 'heart' here, might also be translated as 'bosom' or 'chest' or 'breast'. Jesus is always resting in his Father's bosom, and that is how he makes God known. Thus it is that, when Lazarus dies, Mary says to Jesus not, 'If you had said some prayers... laid your hands on him...' but, 'If you had been here, my brother would not have died' (John 11:32). Being where Jesus is rescues us from death.

Now we come to the last supper, and again the Greek word *kolpon* is used. The beloved disciple is described in most translations as 'reclining next to Jesus' (v. 25), yet the correct translation would be to say that he is resting on Jesus' breast. Not only is this astonishingly intimate, but, as the Gospel draws to a close, it is a clear echo of the first chapter. Jesus rests in the Father's bosom and the beloved disciple rests in Jesus' bosom, that he might see and know God. He is literally being where Jesus is.

Traditionally we associate the beloved disciple with the apostle John, and this may well be a correct association, but perhaps the evangelist avoids giving a name for another reason: the Gospel is about us, whom Jesus calls friends. *We* are now the beloved disciples; we are the disciples whom Jesus loves. It is our task during this Holy Week—and throughout our lives—to be where Jesus is, to be within his body the Church, to receive him in the sacrament of the Eucharist, and to let his words dwell in us. Christ invites us to an amazing intimacy with him: we are to recline on his chest, to rest in his bosom, so that as he is where the Father is, so we may be where he is and so with the Father also.

3 Betrayal

Matthew 26:14–25

What made Judas betray Jesus? Matthew suggests greed, recording that Judas asked how much the chief priests would give him to hand Jesus over (v. 15). It would seem a terrible thing to do for money, yet we know how powerful a force money is and how we are all in thrall to it to an extent—not least if we are under the terrible pressure caused by debt. Perhaps Judas owed money elsewhere and was desperate to find a way to pay it back?

Yet the 30 pieces of silver are not unimportant in themselves: they represent both the price of a slave (Exodus 21:32) and the wage of a shepherd (Zechariah 11:12). Judas, perhaps without realising it, has revealed in his very act of betrayal two aspects of Jesus' mission: his servanthood and his role as the true, good shepherd. Later, when it is too late, Judas will see what he has done and clearly recall the significance of the amount, for he casts the money back into the temple (Matthew 27:5) exactly as the shepherd is instructed to do in Zechariah 11:13.

We might get a further insight into Judas' motivations from his name. There is some evidence that it derives from the Latin *sicarius*, meaning 'dagger man'—a name given to Jewish terrorists in the first century AD. Judas would not have been alone in expecting the Messiah to be a warrior-king who would lead the Israelites to freedom in battle. It may well have been that he joined Jesus' group expecting him to be precisely that kind of leader—a guerrilla who would wage war on the occupying Roman forces—and became increasingly disillusioned when Christ chose the way of peace and forgiveness. Perhaps, for Judas, it was time to dispose of this disappointment of a Messiah and continue the search for the real one?

The honest answer, however, is that we will never know Judas' motivation, and not just because we haven't been told. Evil is impossible to rationalise because, in the final analysis, it is irrational. Evil is not what the world was designed for: it goes against the grain of the universe. This is why no one will ever be able properly to explain the Holocaust, for example. Even when we ourselves act sinfully, we may find ourselves saying that we don't know why we did it or what came over us. It is also why Judas' behaviour will for ever be a terrible mystery to us, as all evil finally is.

4 The Servant King

At one level, it doesn't take much imagination to see what an act of service Jesus' work of foot-washing was. Not many of us would want to begin hosting a dinner party by scrubbing the guests' feet—and even less so in the first-century Middle East, when the dirt and heat of the day would be rather more significant than in our antiseptic times. It was the traditional task of the servant to wash the feet of guests, and here is the one who (in the words of Graham Kendrick's 'Servant King') 'flung stars into space' now on his knees and cherishing the dirtiest part of his creatures' bodies. We could fruitfully devote the rest of our lives to contemplating the wonder of such abasement and humility on God's part. It is not surprising, then, that he deliberately asks them, 'Do you understand what I have done?' (v. 12). It is also unsurprising that Peter cannot understand, speaking perhaps for all of us with his 'Never!' (v. 8). It is probably not only the outrageous upending of natural hierarchy that shocks Peter but also the intimacy of the action. It is unnerving.

Yet there is a further reason why Jesus asks his disciples if they understand. There was one exception to the rule about foot-washing in the first century: that exception involved the people's host, especially if he was a rabbi, as Jesus was. Instead of his disciples or servants washing his feet, his wife would wash them. She would not do it out of servitude but rather because, by marriage, they were one body and no one had the right to touch her husband's feet but her. Jesus, the rabbi, in washing his disciples' feet, therefore points them towards the unity of Christ and his Church, the bridegroom and bride. He behaves as the wife, for he is the Mother out of whom the blood and water of the church will come on the cross, so that disciple and master can both say together on this day when he institutes the Eucharist, 'This is my body.' He is one body with his disciples—he is married to his Church—and so he gives them his Maundy (from the Latin *mandamus*, for 'command'). His new commandment is to love one another as much as bridegroom and bride love one another (13:34).

5 The death of God

John 19:23–30

What is there to say on a day like this? As Charles Wesley wrote in his hymn 'And can it be': ''Tis mystery all: th' Immortal dies.' We should spend some of today in silence, therefore, reflecting that there are no words for the death of the Son of God. This is why so much of Holy Week, in many churches, involves doing things rather than simply thinking or talking: processing with palm branches, washing feet, receiving Holy Communion, kissing or touching a wooden cross. It is also because Jesus, on this day, does something rather than saying very much.

There are lots of theories of the atonement—of precisely what it was that Jesus did on Good Friday. Our reading today presents us with a picture that is not often noticed—one associated with what Jesus is wearing (v. 23). It might seem strange for John to record our Saviour's clothing on an occasion like this. It could almost seem flippant or at least irrelevant; but it is neither. John records the seamless tunic precisely because it is the same as the seamless tunic that the Jewish high priest wore in the temple when he entered the Holy of Holies to make atonement for the sins of Israel (Leviticus 16:4). Remember also the reference to the veil that separated the Holy of Holies from the rest of the temple, which is said to have been torn in two at the time of Jesus' death (Matthew 27:51). The Jerusalem temple was designed as a microcosm of reality, with the main body of the temple representing the material creation and the Holy of Holies, behind the curtain, representing the immaterial heavens. Every year, the high priest, wearing his seamless robe, would go into the Holy of Holies and, after making sacrifice, would then sprinkle the blood of the animal all over the temple, thereby cleansing and renewing the world that it represented from the impurity and sin that had built up. Jesus, who is the great high priest in his seamless tunic, sheds his own blood to restore order to the world. Because it is his blood and not that of an animal, and, moreover, the blood of the Son of God, the sacrifice is made once and for all, and the divide between heaven and earth is removed for ever—hence the tearing of the curtain at his death.

As we enter spring-time, this image of Jesus' work renewing all things should inspire and strengthen us. He comes as the great high priest and, in his love, sheds blood so that the barrier between heaven and earth might be removed once and for all. Thus God takes an utterly senseless murder by an occupying force and uses it as the supreme means of renewing and restoring meaning to the world.

6 The harrowing of hell

1 Peter 3:15b–22

So we reach Holy Saturday, Easter Eve; we are approaching the greatest day of the Christian year, the peak of and springboard for our whole faith. In churches today there is often much cleaning and dusting, sorting out of hymn books and orders of service, polishing and flower-arranging. This is necessary stuff and can't be avoided, yet it shouldn't be allowed to stop us focusing on the meaning of this day. In his first letter, Peter describes Jesus going to preach to the imprisoned spirits, and Holy Saturday is the day when we recall Christ's 'harrowing of hell'. In that event we see Jesus going down to Sheol (the shady place of the dead in Jewish thought) to preach the gospel to those who lived and died before him, often movingly depicted in icons where a white-robed Christ is holding on to the hands of Adam and Eve and lifting them out of hell and death.

The descent of Jesus Christ into hell is one of the most amazing aspects of our faith: it tells us that there is quite literally nowhere God has not been, no level of separation from goodness, truth and beauty that he has not experienced. One of the perennial questions for Christians, therefore, is 'Is there anyone in hell?' We do not know. It is the essence of Christian hope to pray that hell is empty, but we cannot presume, for, given some of the hells-on-earth we created in the 20th century and still create now, it does not seem impossible that someone should turn their back on God for ever, and God has given us our freedom. Yet the descent of the eternal second person of the Trinity into hell on Holy Saturday must give us pause for thought: is it ultimately possible for someone to cut themselves off from God for ever? In this life, many, many people do, but what about eternity? Might the mercy of God reach down even to those who willed damnation for themselves, plucking them, despite themselves, into the heart of love?

A great theologian of the last century, Hans Urs Von Balthasar, said that Holy Saturday was the place of 'hope for the person who, refusing all love, damns himself. Will not the man who wishes to be totally alone, find beside him in Sheol Someone lonelier still, the Son forsaken by the Father, who will prevent him from experiencing his self-chosen hell to the end?' As we look towards tomorrow's empty tomb, let us pray that that may be so.

Guidelines

We've taken a huge amount in over the last two weeks. We have reflected on our sin but also on the lavish love of God; and, in this Holy Week, especially if we've been able to go to church, we may well have joined in the palm processions, the watching and waiting, the foot-washing, the agony of death and hell and, today, the victory of the resurrection. We can't possibly cope with all of this and assimilate and understand it all. The Church knows this, however, which is why, although there are 40 days of Lent, there are 50 days of Easter—right up to Pentecost. Not only are we given a good length of time to make 'Alleluia!' the key signature to our prayer and praise, but the 50 days are a reminder to us that, in the Christian faith, joy always beats sorrow and that celebration and thanksgiving will always have the last word over sin and lament.

We have seen how God comes among us where we are, using what is there, even our pain, as a vehicle for his grace and salvation. So he lifts up poisonous snakes to give life, turns the punishment of crucifixion into a priestly renewal of all creation, and journeys to preach good news to the lowest depths of hell. And if this is all too much, we can relax, for the cycle of the Christian calendar will give us the same journey again next year. Then we shall be able to move a little deeper again into the wonder of God's love as we make our pilgrimage to our heavenly home.

FURTHER READING

Margaret Barker, *Temple Theology: An introduction*, SPCK, 2004.
Timothy Radcliffe OP, *Seven Last Words*, Continuum, 2004.
Rowan Williams, *The Truce of God: Peacemaking in troubled times*, Canterbury Press, 2005.

Isaiah 19—39

The book of Isaiah is complex. Most readers will know the scholarly view that it divides into three major sections, associated with prophets working at different points in history. The chapters we are looking at over the next two weeks form part of the first section, associated with 'Isaiah of Jerusalem', who prophesied during the last 40 years of the eighth century BC. However, although these chapters are largely associated with one prophet, they do not read in an obviously coherent way. The immediate impression is of a jumble of oracles, dealing not only with Judah and Jerusalem but also with the surrounding nations; speaking not only of judgment and disaster but also of redemption and restoration, with contrasting themes seeming to be randomly juxtaposed.

Readers who used the notes on Isaiah 1—12 published in *Guidelines May–August 2011* know that the political situation during this period shifted and evolved. So the book is complex partly because Isaiah's oracles related to changing circumstances and were addressed to different players on the national and international scenes. But scholars also suggest that, within these chapters, there is also later material by other hands, applying Isaiah's themes to new circumstances, decades or even centuries later. No wonder it is hard to make sense of!

There is one part of our allotted portion that *seems* relatively straight-forward: chapters 36—39 form a little chunk of history 'dropped into' the book, dealing with events during Hezekiah's reign. This account (also found in 2 Kings 18:13—20:19 in very similar form) was probably written up two centuries later, yet no doubt based on actual events in which Isaiah had an important role. However, it should be noted that even the history recorded in these chapters may not be as straightforwardly chronological as it seems: many scholars think that 2 Kings and Isaiah take two separate occasions when an Assyrian army threatened Jerusalem and condense them into one. Hence we find some unevenness in the narrative.

To get a handle on things, I shall comment first on this short historical section. Then, we shall look at oracles selected from some of the preceding chapters of Isaiah, seeing them as the kind of messages the prophet typically gave about the political situations that the history describes.

I am using the text of the New Revised Standard Version.

1 Jerusalem in danger

Isaiah 36

This passage vividly catches the confident, arrogant attitude of an Assyrian official (the Rabshakeh) representing Sennacherib's army, which was at the gates of Jerusalem, and the panic-stricken reaction of King Hezekiah's courtiers who had gone out to parley with him, desperate not to have the morale of the city's inhabitants undermined (v. 12).

Assyria, in northern Mesopotamia (now northern Iraq), was the great superpower during this period of Middle Eastern history. Sennacherib (705–681BC) was determined that as many countries as possible should be subject to his empire, and ruthlessly put down revolts. Assyria's nearest rival in power, Egypt, was attempting to gain influence in countries nearby, including Judah, and the passage is set around 703–701BC, when Hezekiah's policy had been to ally Judah with Egypt in order to escape Assyrian overlordship.

Sennacherib had swept south through various vassal kingdoms, asserting authority over them either by bloody means or by sheer intimidation. Moving into Judah, he had conquered many of the towns and villages of the land. 2 Kings 18:14–16 tells us that in response to these events Hezekiah had already attempted to pay him off with a great deal of money, including the contents of the temple's treasury, and gold stripped from its doorposts. But it seems that Sennacherib was not content: he sent his representative with a large army to the gates of Jerusalem, to underline his anger at the Judean pro-Egyptian policy. No wonder the courtiers were terrified at the threat to their city! The Rabshakeh's taunts seemed based on all-too-real triumphs. Then he 'put the knife in' by claiming that it was the Lord who had sent the Assyrians (v. 10), and that it was because Hezekiah had instituted religious reform that the Lord would now desert Judah (v. 7). But the Rabshakeh was overreaching himself, both when he said this and when he went on to claim that the Lord was simply like the gods of all the other nations, and no match for Assyrian might (v. 20).

This chapter illustrates two factors in the political and military scene which were of concern to the prophet Isaiah: firstly, the folly of the Egyptian alliance, and secondly, the arrogance of Assyria and God's judgment upon it.

2 Hezekiah's distress

Isaiah 37:1–13

Hezekiah was a man of some piety. He adopted the outward signs of mourning and took his troubles to the Lord in the temple (v. 1). Although he had been censured by Isaiah for his policies, nevertheless he turned to the prophet to intercede for the nation in crisis.

Looking at the history as told in Isaiah (unlike 2 Chronicles, which treats him as something of a hero: see 32:32), Hezekiah was a man of mixed motives and mingled achievements—like most of us. His appeal to the Lord through Isaiah was based on the Lord's care for his own reputation (v. 4), not on any claim that help was deserved or that God had been obeyed in the past.

Isaiah responded with words of reassurance, prophesying the withdrawal of Sennacherib to Assyria and his eventual bloody downfall (v. 7). We know from Sennacherib's own account of the campaign of 703–701 that he did withdraw—largely because he had imposed his authority and exacted enough tribute from Judah and her neighbours, and he had matters to attend to in the north. And he did, in fact, die a violent death in about 681BC. So, the prophet's words came true both in the short and in the long term.

It may have been later in the same campaign of 703–701, or during another one in the same region (perhaps 13 or 14 years later, if the name of King Tirhakah in the text is accepted as correct), that we find Sennacherib turning from fighting Libnah, one of the towns of Judah, to face a hostile force moving up from north Africa (v. 9). (If the story comes from a second campaign, the historian who is recounting it to us may have constructed verse 8 in order to make a coherent single story out of two separate ones.) The important thing for us to understand is that at least once, but perhaps on more occasions, Assyrian pressure was taken off Judah and Jerusalem, and the assurance of the prophet was vindicated (vv. 10–13).

We are invited, in the way the Bible tells the story, to note the contrast between the proper humility exhibited by Hezekiah and continuing arrogance on the part of the Assyrians.

3 Prayer and prophecy

Again, we see Hezekiah behaving with piety and prayerfulness. It is a vivid image, this spreading out of Sennacherib's threatening letter before the Lord (v. 14). We might do well to follow this example of taking a physical symbol of whatever frightens us and literally 'spreading it out', or holding it up, in the place we associate most with the Lord's presence, as a sign of handing the source of our fear over to God.

The words of Hezekiah's prayer contain formulations typical of the 'Deuteronomic histories' (including 1 and 2 Kings), from which this passage no doubt springs. We may not know exactly how Hezekiah prayed at the time of the events in question, but it is important to the historian to record that he did pray, that he called the Lord's attention to the danger the Assyrians posed and to their defiance of the living God. And Isaiah responded on the Lord's behalf with oracles directed against Sennacherib.

The first oracle (v. 22) takes up the theme of contempt, turning the scorn that the Assyrians had shown for Judah and its God back against them. It is a striking picture: the city whose inhabitants had so recently been experiencing extremes of fear now tosses its head like a derisive girl behind the backs of those who had inspired such terror—a heartening image for the people of Jerusalem.

The second, much longer oracle (vv. 23–29) addresses the blasphemous nature of Sennacherib's arrogance. In his own eyes, he has set himself up as the Lord's equal, all-powerful, able even to match the miracle of the parting of the Red Sea (v. 25). He suffers from delusions of power that the Greeks would have labelled *hubris*, bearing within them the seeds of self-destruction. But Isaiah says more than that *hubris* brings about its own downfall: he claims that everything Sennacherib has done and everything that will happen to him are alike under the control of the God whom he is defying. When Sennacherib conquered cities, it was only by God's purpose (vv. 26–27); and now, equally by God's purpose, he, the enslaver, will find that he is nothing but a slave (or even a beast of burden) of the maker of heaven and earth (v. 29).

4 Prophecy vindicated

Isaiah 37:30–38

We turn from verse to prose. In verses 30–32, the prosaic process of a return to normality after war is the Lord's 'sign' to Hezekiah. After armies have trampled the land, disrupting the sowing season, it follows that the surviving population will have to support itself on self-sown crops. And, with labourers killed or injured, it may take more than one year to re-establish agricultural routine. But, by a third year, normality begins to set in. Just as the self-seeding remnant of old crops provides agricultural continuity, so the remnant of the population eventually establishes new community. Here is human reason for hope. But hope also comes in God's promise of protection for Jerusalem—offered both for the Lord's 'own sake' and 'for the sake of my servant David' (v. 35). Here is constant covenant-love, which goes beyond obvious human hopes of recovery.

Finally, we hear of events that obviously struck the historian as instances of God's intervention and vindication of Isaiah's promises: the mysterious decimation of Sennacherib's army (v. 36) and the tyrant's own eventual bloody demise (v. 38). We are not told whether the decimation of the army happened while it was just outside Jerusalem (in which case it would have been a dramatic fulfilment of the prophet's oracle in verses 33–35) or elsewhere. Nor are we told exactly how it happened. The Greek historian, Herodotus, about 250 years later, told of Sennacherib's army being dramatically defeated in Egypt because a plague of mice came in the night and ate all its bow-strings and the thongs of its shields. Some commentators think that this hints at an attack of bubonic plague, associated with rodents. Perhaps the story in Isaiah is rooted in this event.

On the other hand, there is a tradition in the Psalms of a mysterious and dramatic deliverance of Jerusalem from an army ranged immediately outside it (see Psalms 48:4–8; 76:4–9); maybe these psalms celebrate the event recorded in our passage.

Did it happen, and if so, when? We cannot know for certain. Assyrian annals record no defeat at the gates of Jerusalem. The main significance for the Jewish or Christian reader is in the message of God's faithfulness to his promise and covenant—the rescue of a 'remnant' and the continued treasuring of the house of David.

5 Healed, restored, forgiven

Isaiah 38

'In those days…' (v. 1). Once more, we are in the realm of rather vague chronology. But the story of Hezekiah's illness parallels in one person's life the pattern of Jerusalem's story—in grave danger, yet saved by the Lord 'at the eleventh hour', with the prophet Isaiah as both messenger and agent of the turnaround. Just as, in the last chapter, signs of hope explicable from normal human experience were set alongside a much more mysterious sign, so here, Isaiah's treatment of Hezekiah's boil with a fig poultice, leading to the king's ability once more to visit the temple (v. 21), is set alongside the mysterious sign of the reversal of the sun's passage over the dial of Ahaz—a set of steps, up which a shadow normally climbed during the day (vv. 7–8). (For the modern reader, this particular sign is problematic, implying a truly cosmic miracle. It may be a device of ancient storytelling, suitable to a tale about a king saved 'in the noontide of his days': v. 10.)

The story of Hezekiah's illness and restoration is told with some extra detail in 2 Kings 20, where the king's treatment with the poultice on Isaiah's advice is placed more prominently. But what is missing there is Hezekiah's psalm of praise, which we find in our passage today. This provides an essential ingredient to make sense of the story, for Hezekiah's prose prayer (v. 3) is thoroughly self-justificatory: it cannot explain why God should change his mind about him. But, in the psalm, we have a reference to the Lord casting Hezekiah's sins behind his back (v. 17). This suggests an element of penitence in his prayer and tears, which would account for Isaiah's return to him with a more hopeful message.

Isaiah prophesied both to Jerusalem and to foreign nations, with threats that left room for repentance and the avoidance of disaster. But even beyond that, he also preached oracles of restoration and forgiveness that would come after disaster had befallen them. Hezekiah's recovery symbolises the possibility of a new start with God, even though (as we shall see in the next chapter) there remains a sense of inevitability about the downward path on which Judah had set itself, and the consequences that it would bring.

6 Unreliable friends

Isaiah 39

This is a chapter full of dramatic irony. When the book of Isaiah was compiled in its final form, the prophecy in verses 6 and 7 had already long been fulfilled and would be a state of affairs that loomed large in the reader's consciousness. Indeed, chapter 40, immediately following this one in the final version of the book, is a message of hope addressed to the descendants of those who had suffered the exile in Babylon, which Isaiah of Jerusalem prophesied.

In Hezekiah's day, though, Babylon was a relatively minor power, a long way off, which posed no threat to Judah and Jerusalem. Indeed, it would have seemed a natural ally in resistance to Assyrian hegemony in the Middle East. What we seem to have, therefore, in the story of Hezekiah's conducted tour of his treasury and armoury for the Babylonian envoys, is an account of a king showing off to another, friendly power. (It is not unknown, even in modern times, for foreign visitors to be treated to military parades and displays of wealth.)

But Isaiah of Jerusalem embodied an austere and uncompromising message from God: security does not rest in what a nation possesses and can 'show off', and the peace of Jerusalem depends not on foreign alliances but on faithfulness to God alone. The prophet foresaw the day when lack of this faithfulness would lead to enslavement by the very nation that Hezekiah was trying to impress. This day was relatively far off (it came in 587BC, more than 100 years after Hezekiah's reign), and Hezekiah would probably have understood Isaiah's threats to refer not to his own, immediate sons, but to more remote descendants—as, indeed, they did. Hezekiah's time as king came to be seen as successful, both in civil and religious terms, with real achievements and desirable reforms (see 2 Kings 20:20 and 2 Chronicles 32:32). Nevertheless, the clouds were gathering on the horizon, even then.

The very last words of the chapter offer us a sharp challenge: how far are we like Hezekiah, living for today and seeing the fate of future generations as too remote for us to be concerned with? Do we have an appropriate sense of urgency about the clouds on our world's horizon?

Guidelines

The book of Isaiah tells of a small nation and its relationship with its neighbours and with the regional superpowers of its day. When we think about our own country's place in the world, we tend not to look for religious prophets to tell us what our nation's policies should be, but rather reflect on the comments of political experts, journalists, historians and other pundits of varying shades of opinion.

Why the difference? Is it because:

• the history we are living through is not 'sacred' history, in the sense that the history of Israel and Judah was?
• we live in a secular society in which a claim to prophesy about current events in the name of God would simply 'cut no ice' with our contemporaries?
• our culture's experience of people claiming to be 'prophets' or 'religiously inspired' in their view of politics is tainted by the way in which such people have seemed or seem to be intolerant, unbalanced, dangerous or crazy (for example, in the era of the English Civil War or in the circles of extreme Islamists or religiously inspired West Bank settlers today)?

Whatever the reason for the disappearance of prophecy in our modern evaluation of political events, it leaves Christians with the challenge of trying to discern God's will and presence in the wider world. To what extent might the following themes in Isaiah help us in this discernment?

• A challenge to the idea that 'realpolitik' should determine whom we choose as allies—or whether we should involve ourselves in military alliances at all.

- The fatal danger of arrogance in a nation's view of itself.
- An understanding that repentance is relevant not just for individuals but for nations, too.
- A belief that God is ultimately in control of events, whoever seems to be most powerful, humanly speaking.
- A conviction that prayer has a significant role to play, even in the affairs of nations.
- The gift of finding hope, both in 'natural' and apparently 'supernatural' patterns of events.

Even though we may not look for individual 'prophets' today in national life, in the sense of people like Isaiah, Christians often talk about 'taking a prophetic stance' on this issue or that. What does the figure of Isaiah, as we see him relating to Hezekiah and his dilemmas, tell us about what it means to take a 'prophetic stance'?

1 Futility of the Egyptian alliance

Isaiah 20 and 31

By the time of the events we read about last week, Isaiah had long been counselling against alliance with Egypt. Isaiah 20:1 refers to 711BC—ten years before King Sennacherib's first campaign and threat to Jerusalem. Ashdod was a city of the Philistines, who lived along the coastal strip to the west of Judah. Their alliance with Egypt let them down in the face of Assyrian might. Isaiah's prophetic action, in walking barefoot and naked (or at least, without a coat) around Jerusalem for three years, was intended to spell out to Hezekiah the folly of making a similar mistake: Egypt would be ignominiously defeated by Assyria, despite its new and seemingly vigorous dynasty of Ethiopian kings. This defeat did, in fact, take place in 701BC, during Sennacherib's victorious campaign.

But was Isaiah's consistent message that Judah should not ally itself with Egypt (see also 19:1–7; 30:1–7) simply based on the intuition (or inspired knowledge) that relying on the southern superpower against the northern one would mean 'backing the wrong horse'? Chapter 31 suggests a deeper argument: reliance on Egypt meant reliance on outward signs of military strength (v. 1), misplacing trust that should be placed in God alone (v. 3). It was a part of a fundamental betrayal of the covenant (v. 6). Of course, Egypt had particular significance: it was from her clutches that the Israelites had escaped in their foundational march to freedom. To choose alliance with Egypt would, therefore, be 'going back'—embracing as saviours the very war horses and chariots whose predecessors had pursued the Israelites into the Red Sea. The particular irony of sending treasure back across the wilderness to buy the protection of those whom they had despoiled in the exodus was not lost on Isaiah (30:6). But chapter 31 hints at a more general message, which may be relevant to us: alliances, even with those who have the best technology, are no substitute for the righteousness of God's ways in a nation's policies. Clearly, Isaiah is not promoting a totally pacifist philosophy here—the picture of God himself fighting for his people is too violent for that—but he is advocating a kind of radical trust that calls into question the calculations of realpolitik.

2 The downfall of arrogance

Isaiah 28:14–22

In chapters 36 and 37 we heard of the arrogance of Assyria, but arrogance in the face of God was not the sin of that nation alone. Even the Hebrews could be guilty of it. The first part of chapter 28 (vv. 1–13) condemns the pride of Ephraim (that is, the northern kingdom, Israel), which was punished by its fall to the Assyrians in 722BC; but from verse 14 onwards Isaiah turns his focus upon the 'scoffing' people of Jerusalem and Judah, threatening them with an 'overwhelming scourge' passing through to punish them (v. 18). The 'covenant with death' mentioned in verses 15 and 18 may be an allegorical way of speaking about Judah's alliance with Egypt, but it is couched in language that suggests vast overconfidence, rooted in deep spiritual malaise. Verses 19 and 20 picture the consequences of this arrogance—punishment beating down upon the people day after day, leading to an understanding of the prophet's message so clear that it will no longer be possible to bury one's head in the blankets and ignore it. Set in stark contrast to the people's folly is the solid faithfulness of God (vv. 16–17).

Elsewhere in the oracles of this first part of Isaiah, we find other condemnations of the pride and arrogance of different nations—Moab (16:6), Egypt (19:11–13), Tyre (23:7–9), and particularly Babylon (14:12–15). The passage about Babylon is a specially eloquent condemnation of the spiritual arrogance of a nation and its king. It is probably an oracle dating from a time much later than that of Isaiah of Jerusalem. Nevertheless, it is firmly in his tradition of condemning whole nations—his own included—for the sin of arrogance. It is a key part of his tradition to assert the Lord's sovereignty over all peoples, and to see every policy and claim to glory which does not acknowledge that sovereignty as being rooted in poisonous and self-destructive pride.

This raises the question for us as to what constitutes 'pride and arrogance' in the affairs of nations today. Are there ways in which it still makes sense to speak of nations as either 'arrogant' or 'humble', without the framework of theocracy as a vision of how they should be ruled?

3 Complacency rather than penitence

Isaiah 22:1–14

Arrogance has a close relative in complacency. This oracle was probably addressed to the people of Jerusalem in 701BC, when much of Judah had been devastated but Jerusalem spared. (However, verses 5–8a may have been rewritten to apply the original prophecy to the situation 120 years later, when the Babylonians invaded.) We are invited to contrast exultant celebrations in the city (vv. 1–2) with the prophet's lament over what had happened in the surrounding country (v. 4). The term used for 'valley' in the phrase 'the valley of vision' denotes a steep ravine, such as those that surround Jerusalem, forming its natural defence, by contrast with the word for a broad valley (as in v. 7). It is as though the vision of the inhabitants of Jerusalem was narrowed down to concern for their own small patch alone. Equally, for all the elaborate procedures taken for the defence of their city (vv. 8b–11), they neglected to repair their relationship with God in the way that the prophet was calling for. The ravaging of Judah's other cities and towns should have led to national repentance (v. 12) but, instead, was disregarded, and metropolitan celebrations were held (albeit in a somewhat fatalistic frame of mind, if the proverb in verse 13 conveys the thoughts of the people rather than an ironic comment by the prophet).

Perhaps, given Isaiah's own prophecies about the Lord's defence of Jerusalem, it would have been surprising if its inhabitants had not considered it a special case, rejoicing in what they saw as divine inviolability. Yet Isaiah preached not only God's ultimate commitment to the city but also his threats of punishment for the people's unfaithfulness. The two parts of the message, ostensibly in tension, belong together. Trust in God's promises should be translated into neither complacency nor reliance on human ingenuity. The threat of 'no forgiveness' for these attitudes in verse 14 has a terrible sense of finality about it, and is cast in a form suggesting that here the prophet uttered what he heard from divine dictation.

The final challenge to complacency was supplied by whoever edited Isaiah, placing this oracle concerning Jerusalem within a series of threatening prophecies directed at foreign nations. By implication, Jerusalem is judged on the same footing as they are.

4 God is in charge

Isaiah 29:1–16

The Lord is in charge of the attack on Jerusalem; the Lord is in charge of the sudden defeat of her enemies; the Lord is in charge of hardening the hearts and blinding the eyes of his people; the Lord is in charge of all that happens, as a potter is of the clay. This is the message of these oracles.

Isaiah stresses the strangeness of God's actions to human beings (as in 28:21), firstly by addressing Jerusalem by a name not known elsewhere—Ariel. This word probably means 'altar hearth' but it also sounds, in Hebrew, like the word for 'lion of God' or 'hero'. The pun is probably meant to be paradoxical. Jerusalem, the centre of the heroic Davidic kingdom, is reminded that David himself once besieged her (when he defeated the Jebusites, v. 3); and now David's God encamps against her. She is almost like a sacrifice on the altar in her prostration (vv. 1–4), but then suddenly becomes the place where the Lord sends down fire from heaven (v. 6, as in Elijah's conflict with the prophets of Baal) to make her misery disappear like a nightmare (v. 7) and discomfit those who fight against her.

The next two oracles take up the theme of the hardening of hearts from the account of Isaiah's call in 6:10: 'Make the mind of this people dull, and stop their ears, and shut their eyes, so that they may not look with their eyes, and listen with their ears, and comprehend with their minds, and turn and be healed.' This passage, given in the Gospels as Jesus' explanation of the purpose of parables (see Matthew 13:14–15; Mark 4:12; Luke 8:10), is one that we find difficult. Here in Isaiah 29, however, we find some explanation for the blinding of eyes and stupefying of understanding, as being the penalty for hypocritical worship (v. 13). Isaiah continues to emphasise the strangeness of God's actions in verse 14, by repeating that God's deeds are 'amazing'—that is, beyond human wisdom.

The last oracle in our passage enjoys the irony of pitting human beings who think they're too clever for God against his ultimate control of us (vv. 15–17). It is not we who turn things upside down: that is what he does!

5 Prayer and salvation

Isaiah 33

In the final form of the book of Isaiah, this chapter comes at the halfway point, acting in some respects as a hinge. It is full of language taken up from the earlier oracles in the book, though often reworked and given a radically new significance, sometimes quite contrary to what went before. For example, verse 24 takes up the word 'sick' from 1:5 and the word 'forgiven' from 22:14, this time to prophesy healing and remission of sins rather than doom and condemnation.

The chapter is also full of concepts that we find in the Psalms; in particular, verse 15 is reminiscent of the portrait of the ideal worshipper in Psalm 15, while the picture of Zion as a city of 'broad rivers and streams' in verse 21 reminds us of Psalm 46:4: 'There is a river whose streams make glad the city of God, the holy habitation of the Most High.' (Jerusalem is, geographically, *not* a city on a river, but depends on conduits for its water supply!)

Whether this chapter is original to Isaiah of Jerusalem is debated, but it certainly grows out of his thinking. In Assyria, Judah had faced a mighty 'destroyer' (v. 1), a people of a stammering speech (see 28:11), who had apparently been made to flee in some miraculous way from Jerusalem, as in verse 3. We find here Isaiah's paradoxical interplay between, on the one hand, God's wrath at Jerusalem's sins (v. 14) and her breaking of the covenant (v. 8) and, on the other, his mysterious and effective commitment to her salvation (vv. 17–24). In this chapter, the latter side of the paradox comes out more strongly, leading some of the prophet's earlier threatening language to be turned to a new end.

The key to this turning seems to be that in this chapter, the people themselves have 'turned': they are praying. 'O Lord, be gracious to us; we wait for you…' (v. 2) is a prayer of intercession; 'The Lord is our judge, the Lord is our ruler, the Lord is our king; he will save us' (v. 22) is a prayer of obedient confidence.

Isaiah tells us that events, even in the life of nations, can 'turn' on humble prayer, especially if it is allied with faithful lives (as in v. 15), a living prayer in themselves.

6 Hope, natural and supernatural

Isaiah 28:23–29 and 19:18–24

We saw last week that Isaiah drew on agricultural life as a source of hope (see comments on Isaiah 37:30–38). In 28:23–29 we find another example of the same thinking: couching his prophecy in the form of the 'Wisdom tradition' (as in Proverbs), he speaks about the processes of ploughing, harrowing, sowing and threshing. Ploughing, harrowing and threshing are all violent actions, and are symbols of God's approaching punishment (the oracle immediately prior to this one ended, 'I have heard a decree of destruction from the Lord God of hosts upon the whole land': 28:22). However, none of these processes will be endless or inappropriately extreme, and they are all directed towards bringing in the harvest. So, the wisdom of the farmer points to the wisdom of God in his treatment of his people. Destruction is paradoxically directed to a constructive end; beyond it, there is hope.

The last part of chapter 19 shows just how all-embracing this hope can be from God's supernatural perspective. The two great powers with which Isaiah's prophecies are concerned are seen no longer as enemies, alien to the Lord and each other, but as fellow worshippers with the children of Israel, and united by a highway. Although other oracles foresee a time when different nations will turn to Judah for shelter (the Moabites: 16:3–4) and come to Jerusalem in worship (the Ethiopians: 18:7), the vision of God's loving relationship with Egypt and Assyria in 19:24–25, on a par with his love for Israel, is of a different order. Note, too, that the Egyptians will have places to worship God in their own land.

Some commentators believe that these verses originated at a time much later than Isaiah's (for example, the third century BC), and that they refer to the growth of Jewish settlements and worship in the diaspora. However, although this might explain the focus on Egypt, the inclusion of Assyria in a much later prophecy would be puzzling, since the Assyrian empire and its capital, Nineveh, were destroyed in 612BC. We have seen in our reading of Isaiah's oracles how startling they can be in their reversal of expectations; perhaps we can accept this vision of ultimate reconciliation, although it has never been fulfilled, as our concluding lesson from his message.

Guidelines

When Christians discuss passages from the Old Testament dealing with God's faithfulness to his people and love for Jerusalem, there may be an unspoken question about how they relate to the contemporary situation in the Middle East.

Christians—like Jews—differ sharply among themselves as to whether prophecies such as Isaiah's are relevant in understanding the place of the modern state of Israel in God's purposes. It is an agonising issue because, humanly speaking, the communities in the holy land seem irreconcilable, and so much bitterness is entrenched in the situation. However we personally see it, we must acknowledge that other faithful believers (including Jewish and Arab Christians) see things very differently from us. What can unite us is prayer—simply holding the situation before God, asking for light for all concerned and the peace that only he can give. The following words could be a vehicle for such prayer:

Pray for the peace of Jerusalem:
'May they prosper who love you.
Peace be within your walls,
and security within your towers.'
For the sake of my relatives and friends
I will say, 'Peace be within you.'
For the sake of the house of the Lord our God,
I will seek your good. (Psalm 122:6–9)

This particular question about the relationship of ancient prophecy to modern politics points to wider ones. In what sense does prophecy fore-tell the future? What kind of fulfilment of prophecy validates it?

We have seen in Isaiah 19—39 that some oracles were apparently fulfilled in subsequent history; about others we cannot be so sure, and others, still, have clearly never found fulfilment. As Christians, we are used to thinking of Jesus as the fulfilment of prophecy, yet we know how he confounded the messianic expectations of his own people, who were very familiar with the prophetic books. This should suggest that when we read them, even having unravelled what there is to know about their historical context and motivation, there is still a good deal of mystery about what their oracles meant and mean. Even so, these puzzling reflections entice us with the conviction that God is and has been mysteriously involved in the affairs of our world, calling each age to be alert to the strangeness of his deeds and to remain faithful in its response.

FURTHER READING

Jo Bailey Wells, *Isaiah* (The People's Bible Commentary), BRF, 2006. A devotional commentary, based on sound scholarship.

John Goldingay, *Isaiah* (New International Bible Commentary), Hendrickson/Paternoster Press, 2001. A scholarly commentary.

John Sawyer, *Isaiah* (two vols.) (The Daily Study Bible), Westminster John Knox Press/St Andrew Press, 1986 and subsequent editions. A scholarly commentary intended for popular use.

2 Timothy, Titus and Philemon

Over the coming week we shall be looking at 2 Timothy, Titus and Philemon, three of the pastoral epistles of Paul (although, arguably, all of Paul's epistles could be described as pastoral: see *Paul as Pastor* by Patrick Whitworth, BRF, 2012). Each of these letters is addressed to a named person—two with pastoral responsibilities for churches (Timothy and Titus) and the third a Christian owner of slaves, Philemon, to whom Paul is sending back the runaway slave Onesimus, who has been radically converted after contact with Paul in gaol.

Timothy was a long-term associate of Paul, whom he first met in Lystra, perhaps when Timothy was around the age of 16. He was of mixed parentage, his father being Greek and his mother Jewish. Timothy travelled with Paul on his second missionary journey, visiting Philippi, Thessalonica, Berea, Athens and Corinth. He later returned with Paul to Ephesus for Paul's three-year ministry there and undertook visits to the churches in Macedonia and Corinth for Paul (see Acts 19:21–22; 1 Corinthians 16:10–11). Latterly he joined Paul in Rome during the years of Paul's house arrest, before being sent to Ephesus as Paul's delegate and as a pastor of the church there (around AD64). It is as a church leader, therefore, that Timothy receives Paul's letters of encouragement and instruction for his ministry.

Titus was also an associate of Paul. A more robust person than Timothy, he was given the difficult tasks of organising the collection for the church in Judea at Corinth and generally acting as intermediary in Paul's frequently stormy relationship with the Corinthian church. He was sent to Crete as the pastor and leader of the church, and it was there that he received Paul's letter of pastoral instruction.

Lastly, Philemon, quite possibly from Colosse, was a wealthy Christian slave owner. Probably personally known to Paul, he is instructed by Paul, in an exquisite little letter, to receive Onesimus back as a brother in the Lord and to treat him as such rather than as a runaway slave deserving punishment.

In reading these epistles, we could consider the following questions. What guiding principles about leadership were given to these men, each of whom was in a position of pastoral responsibility? What were the special characteristics called for by Paul, which should mark out the Christian leader or pastor? Which issues raised by Paul in this correspondence are especially current today?

Unless otherwise indicated, quotations are taken from the New International Version of the Bible.

1 Fan the flame, guard the deposit

2 Timothy 1:1–18

We are very fortunate to have a proper fireplace in our sitting-room and, on most Sundays in winter, we have a log fire in the afternoon. As the fire dies down, the embers often need fanning into flame with bellows to encourage the fire and prevent it from dying out: more air and more fuel are usually needed.

Paul says as much, in a spiritual sense, to Timothy. He recalls Timothy's past and the roots of his faith: his mother's and grandmother's faith (v. 5) and their example and instruction of him from an early age. They laid the fire. Paul also recalls a moment of profound prayer when he laid hands on Timothy, commissioning him perhaps for his work in Ephesus and gifting him for this ministry (v. 6). A new spark was given. But Paul also recalls Timothy's tears, perhaps exhibiting anxiety at the responsibility given to him (v. 4). In view of these things—his well-grounded faith, his gifting and his vulnerable nature—Paul urges him to fan the flame of his faith and gifting, for we are called to serve not with 'a spirit of timidity, but a spirit of power, of love and of self-discipline' (v. 7).

More air and more fuel are needed to sustain the fire of passion for God's kingdom. How do we fan into flame God's gifts to us? And what is the fuel that we can add to the fire of faith in our lives?

We must not avoid any hardship or suffering that may be part of faithful service. Paul is in prison and urges Timothy not to be ashamed of what has befallen him. The gospel is worth suffering for, says Paul. It centres on Jesus, who has destroyed death and brought 'life and immortality to light through the gospel' (v. 10, NRSV). Paul is a herald, apostle and teacher of the gospel, and is convinced that God will guard what has been entrusted to him. His investment of time, effort and even health in the kingdom will never be a wasted investment: his stock will soar. Timothy, take heart!

Lastly Timothy is to protect the deposit of teaching that has been given him, with guard-dogs of faith and love—those Pauline twins that are the essence of a healthy spiritual life. We must guard the deposit of sound teaching with the help of the Holy Spirit.

If you have any pastoral responsibilities, what do you need to do to fan the flame of your gifting, to be able to bear with difficulties, knowing that the outcome will not be in vain, or to guard the deposit with the help of the Holy Spirit?

2 Avoid some things and seize hold of others

2 Timothy 2:1–26

I remember, as a young man, once lingering by a postbox (well before the days of the internet or mobile phones), wondering whether to send a letter to a girl. She was not yet a Christian, but I was hoping for some kind of relationship with her. Rightly or wrongly, these words of Paul came to mind: 'No one serving as a soldier gets involved in civilian affairs' (2:4). Nevertheless, I posted the letter. She did not respond, although she became a Christian later.

The point that Paul makes here is that a leader especially must be single-minded, like a soldier who is hardened by service and seeking to please his commanding officer, or an athlete training hard and competing according to the rules, or a hardworking farmer. Single-mindedness, competing fairly and hard work are important qualities in Christian leadership. Paul has gone to prison because his faith in Jesus includes those qualities.

Likewise, there are things to avoid. Paul's list includes godless chatter or misinformed talk, like that of Hymenaeus and Philetus (who were saying that the resurrection of believers had already taken place: v. 18). Its effect is compared to gangrene, which can only be checked by amputation. Then there are the evil desires of youth (v. 22; what might they be?) and 'stupid arguments' (v. 23).

The effective pastor, by contrast, is one who pursues 'righteousness, faith, love and peace' (v. 22), who 'gently instructs' his opponents (v. 25) and 'must be kind to everyone, able to teach, not resentful' (v. 24). All of that sounds like a great challenge.

Is this your idea of a pastoral leader? If you have pastoral responsibilities, what areas might you need to work on? We can be, Paul suggests (vv. 20–21), either like an old pewter mug in the house or like a gleaming gold bowl. It seems that what we are depends largely on what we do: we are told that must 'cleanse ourselves'. A chorus or rhyme to strengthen us might be like the one we find in verses 11–13. Armed with such thoughts, we could endure anything. In any case, nothing can chain down God's word (v. 9b).

3 Final thoughts

2 Timothy 3—4

Paul is nearing the end of his life: he says, 'I have fought the good fight, I have finished the race, I have kept the faith' (4:7). He had been under house arrest (see Acts 28:30), and later he was imprisoned, awaiting trial or execution (see Philippians 1:13), probably during the reign of Nero, in around AD64. With this urgency in mind, he prepares Timothy for life after Paul.

Paul is realistic about the challenges ahead (see 3:1–9). The marks of the coming age will be brashness, greed, selfishness, violence, pursuit of pleasure, and deceit. Could we use the same list to describe society today? What evidence would you cite?

In the face of this immoral onslaught, Timothy must be robust. Paul hardly paints a picture of coming ease; rather, Timothy should expect to encounter the sort of experiences that Paul himself faced in the towns of Timothy's native country—in Pisidian Antioch, Iconium and Lystra (Timothy's home town: see Acts 16:1), where Paul was all but stoned to death (14:19b). Paul hands down the sobering one-liner that 'all who want to live a godly life in Christ Jesus will be persecuted' (2 Timothy 3:12). In the face of this, Timothy must continue in what he has learned and rely on inspired, God-breathed scripture. Keep steady, Timothy; keep being inspired and trained by scripture!

Finally, Timothy is not only to keep reading and remembering (3:14) but also to keep ministering at all times—preaching, teaching, remaining patient and faithful. Difficulties will come and disappointment will be round the corner, but he must keep going

Despite his endurance of so many hardships, Paul too was human: he needed friends, his cloak and his parchments (4:13); he needed people to stand by him. But the core of his life was the knowledge that 'the Lord stood at my side and gave me strength' (4:17). Are we pinning our hopes on him? If so, we will not be disappointed.

4 Straightening out the unfinished

Titus 1:1–16

Although the title above is an obvious mixed metaphor—for you complete what is left unfinished, and straighten out what is crooked—the phrase is the more vivid for its rough-hewn quality. Titus had the job of taking the church in Crete forward to greater maturity. Crete, which Paul visited briefly on his voyage to Rome (Acts 27:7–12) but had no time to evangelise, may have been subsequently revisited and evangelised by him between the time of his house arrest in Rome and his final imprisonment. In any event, Titus, Paul's trusted companion, emissary to the Corinthian church and more robust church leader than Timothy, was put in charge pastorally in Crete.

It is not far-fetched to think that Titus gained invaluable experience by being Paul's emissary in his sensitive and difficult relationship with the Corinthians. He had to bring them Paul's reproach for their slowness in concluding the collection for the poor Christians in Judea (see 2 Corinthians 8:1–7). This would have been a learning experience for Titus and, no doubt, helpful in preparing him for future leadership of a church and the problems that sometimes need to be confronted. Furthermore, it seems that Titus was well chosen by Paul as an envoy: he appears to have relished the travel and the opportunity to meet the Corinthians, and had confidence in his abilities under God's grace to represent Paul and extract a positive response. Paul says of him, 'He is coming to you with much enthusiasm and on his own initiative' (2 Corinthians 8:17b). Is there someone to whom you could give valuable experience in leadership which would develop their gifts and confidence further?

The situation Titus faced was of a 'rebellious people' (v. 10) with a tendency to lie (pervasive in Crete: v. 12) and an enjoyment of Jewish myths (v. 14), and a Judaising 'out with the knife' circumcision party. How do you 'straighten out' that lot? Robustly, it would seem, so Titus was the right man for the job. 'They must be silenced,' counselled Paul (v. 11).

Furthermore, good leaders needed to be appointed. A good leader is admirably described in verses 8 and 9. Qualities such as hospitality, good family living (v. 6), self-control and faithfulness 'to the trustworthy message' are picked out. In other words, character is all-important. In an age when people are obsessed with what they look like, Paul says that what really matters is what we *are* like.

Is there anything that we are being called to straighten out or complete? If so, how will we set about it? Which qualities promote the church's unity and well-being and which qualities quickly destroy it (see v. 7)?

5 The trickle-down effect

Titus 2—3

A cascade is a lovely thing! Generally we think of it in terms of water falling over a rock formation, whether natural or artificial. Here, the source of the spiritual waterfall or cascade is beautifully described in Titus 3:4–7. Paul speaks of 'renewal by the Holy Spirit, whom [God the Father] poured out on us generously through Jesus Christ' (vv. 5–6). This is an example of trinitarian blessing in which each person of the Godhead initiates and promotes a cascade of grace and mercy.

The fourth-century Cappadocian fathers called this interaction 'perichoresis'. Perichoresis literally means to 'dance around', as if the Trinity were involved in a beautiful, controlled, purposeful and carefully choreographed dance. The Cappadocians had the notion that each member of the Trinity was utterly involved in the work of the others, so that each was involved in creation, redemption, sanctification and re-creation. None is a bystander, simply admiring passively the divine work of the others and giving well-deserved applause; no, each was and is fully involved in the work of the others, bringing it to either painful or beautiful conclusion. So Paul's blessing is one more example of each member of the Trinity dancing to a tune of blessing of which we are the unworthy recipients. How good is that?

But what is the outcome? Surprisingly, the answer appears to be 'self-control'. The older men are to be self-controlled (2:2); the older women must teach the younger to be self-controlled (v. 5); the young men, not so surprisingly, are called to be self-controlled (v. 6) and, in summary, Paul says that the cascading grace of God results in our saying 'No' to ungodliness and living self-controlled lives (v. 12). What does this self-control look like? It does not result in impassionate, wooden, unexciting lives but lives that are rid of selfish passion and instead suffused with a passion for mercy, truth and love. The aim is to be passionate for those qualities but controlled about our own selfish desires.

The cascade is God's grace, and, as it trickles down over the structure of the church community, it transforms, cleanses and makes glisten our otherwise selfish lives. Grace leading to this kind of self-control is the Cretan model for church. Is it ours?

6 Slavery

Philemon

This is a short but exquisite letter, written with infinite delicacy, about a problem that loomed large in the Roman Empire—slavery. It has been estimated that in the Roman Empire there were several million slaves. In every city, almost half the population would have been slaves. The slave rebellion led by Spartacus (numbering 70,000) was repressed with the utmost cruelty: slaves were crucified all along the Appian Way to Rome, in an avenue of cruel, vindictive repression.

Against that background, Paul sends back to Philemon a slave who has become a Christian. The slave, Onesimus, has been punished and could be further punished, but for Paul all people are equal—and especially so in Christ. His famous dictum 'There is neither Jew nor Gentile, neither slave nor free, neither male nor female, for you are all one in Christ Jesus' (Galatians 3:28) abolishes all barriers of status, including that between master and slave. But how is such equality to be implemented? By a modern-style political campaign, in an empire governed by a dictatorship? Unlikely! By a press campaign based on graffiti? Impossible! No, for Paul, slavery had to be dissolved by fellowship, not disbanded by armed rebellion.

So Paul identifies intimately with Onesimus: he is 'my very heart' (v. 12) and 'very dear to me' (v. 16b). He urges Philemon, 'Welcome him as you would welcome me' (v. 17). In this way, Paul hopes, he can persuade Philemon to regard Onesimus differently. He prefers to gain Philemon's approval of and favour for Onesimus freely, spontaneously and without any compulsion (vv. 9, 14). In this way there may develop a genuine mutual regard for each other and a lasting change. Slavery may still exist, but this could be the first step towards freedom.

It took thousands of years to ban slavery in the so-called free world. Through the efforts of William Wilberforce and his friends, the slave trade was eventually ended in Britain and its colonies early in the 19th century; in the US, it was some 50 or so years later. But we know from the work of Stop the Traffik (www.stopthetraffik.org) that slavery still goes on, right under our noses—not least in the trafficking of young women for sexual abuse. Like Paul, we must work wherever we can for its ending and the knowledge that each person is potentially 'a dear brother' or sister (v. 16).

Guidelines

Paul's vast experience and wisdom as a Christian leader are evident in his pastoral letters, along with his fatherly concern for the recipients and the churches they lead. These men, Timothy, Titus and Philemon, are clearly his trusted colleagues in ministry, and Paul writes to each one personally—not trying to force a set of blanket rules and regulations on them but tailoring his instructions and encouragement to their own personalities and the specific situations that they face.

If you have pastoral or other leadership responsibilities, think of and pray for your own ministerial colleagues. What particular instructions and encouragement might they need at this time? Whether you have such responsibilities or not, consider what you might learn about interpersonal relationships from Paul's letters to his fellow workers in Christ.

Isaac's journeys

I have always felt a certain sympathy for Isaac. Sandwiched between his father Abraham and his son Jacob, Isaac occupies much the same position as the child unfavourably compared with an older sibling in school, or the church leader who has tried to fill the overlarge shoes of a saintly, wise and beloved predecessor. If you know what it is like to feel second-best, you will empathise with Isaac.

Many commentators make the point that Isaac did not achieve much in his life. Although he lived longer than either his father or his son, Isaac never left Canaan and never received a new name from God. Abraham, Jacob and Joseph have around twelve chapters of the Bible each, devoted to their exploits. Only one chapter (Genesis 26) has Isaac as the major focus, and in that chapter he seems to repeat many of the exploits of his father. Nevertheless, when the Bible traces the lineage of the Israelites, it invokes the names of 'Abraham, Isaac and Jacob'. Isaac is the child of promise, the child of hope, the one to whom was entrusted the continuation of God's covenant with Abraham. And Isaac's story is all the more powerful because he is depicted 'warts and all', with his weaknesses as well as his strengths laid out.

Our focus for this series will be Genesis 26, a chapter that brings together many stories about Isaac and his exploits in the Philistine valley of Gerar. The chapter is built around Isaac's relations with the Philistine king Abimelek and is bracketed by two near-identical blessings that Isaac received from God. As we study Genesis 26, we will intersperse readings from that chapter with other passages from the Bible that develop the theme.

Unless otherwise indicated, quotations are taken from the NIV.

1 When God says, 'Stay'

Genesis 26:1–6

Genesis 26 is full of images of water and drought. As a semi-nomad, Isaac would have been used to following the flocks away from areas of drought and famine and settling in areas where water was more plentiful. In this case, famine drove him to Gerar, where Abimelek was king. Probably he intended this to be a stopping-place on the way down to Egypt, whose Nile-fed fields made it a safe refuge in times of famine. His father Abraham had stayed in both Gerar (Genesis 20:1) and Egypt (12:20). However, Isaac's stay in Gerar lasted longer than he anticipated, for God's command to him was to 'stay'. In fact, he stayed in Gerar for 'a long time' (v. 8), long enough to settle down. But there is a sense in which he was sidelined. He was neither in the place of promise (Canaan) nor in the place of security (Egypt).

We live in a world that is driven by novelty. Advertisers sell products by making us dissatisfied with what we have and encouraging us to desire something 'new' or 'improved'. Even in church, we may be bombarded with the lessons of the latest success story or the revelations of the latest bestseller. While a certain amount of dissatisfaction with the status quo is needed for progress, what happens to us in this climate when God's word to us is 'Stay'? It can be a hard and frustrating word to obey, especially if the place where we find ourselves is not a place of promise or plenty or security.

It is interesting that, as God commanded Isaac to stay in Gerar, he also restated the promise that he had given to Abraham—a promise of his presence and blessing, and the promise of descendants. This promise is repeated or clarified many times in Genesis. Abraham received the promise over and over again in chapters 13, 15, 17, 21 and 22, but this was the first time God spoke to Isaac. Perhaps Isaac needed reassurance that while he might have felt sidelined, he was not forgotten, and that the promise he carried with him throughout his life was still true.

2 God's plans and ours

Acts 16:6–10

The apostle Paul was a strategic thinker. Several times in the book of Acts and in the epistles, we see evidence of his plans and his hopes (for example, Acts 19:21). In Romans 15:28, we learn that his travel plans included a trip to Spain. Similarly, in individual missionary journeys, Paul displayed a clear strategic brain. He sought out key population and trade centres, often choosing cities with a large Jewish population who might be receptive to the gospel.

People with such defined plans can often be inflexible, unable to adapt to changing circumstances or new information. However, Paul was not one of them. Several times he had to change and adapt. Here in Acts 16, he moves the whole focus of his mission from Asia Minor to mainland Greece, after seeing a vision of a Macedonian man calling him there. This move demanded a change of focus as well as a geographical and cultural change. Previously, Paul and Silas had been essentially strengthening existing churches and building up the disciples (15:36, 41). Now they were again called to plant new churches in a new territory.

This crossing into Europe was prefaced by a period that must have been greatly frustrating. Paul was prevented from preaching in the provinces of Asia (v. 6) and Bithynia (v. 7), and gradually seemed to be steered to Troas, a natural crossing-place into Europe. Clarity came only when the divine plan was confirmed by the vision that Paul received in verse 9.

With this new focus came new companions. Disagreement with Barnabas over the selection of the team had led to a parting of their ways. To strengthen his depleted team, Paul recruited Timothy, whose father was Greek (16:1). Also joining Paul for the first time at this point was another Greek—Luke, the author of Acts. Although this is not directly stated, we can see how the text changes from third person to first person plural in verse 10. The formation of a new team and the choice of companions doubtless proved key as the party crossed into Europe.

There are, perhaps, two main lessons to learn from the experience of Paul in our passage today. The first is that God is in control. It is good for us to plan and to have hopes and aspirations, but that should not make us closed to the possibility that God has other plans. The second lesson is that God does not say 'No' for the sake of saying 'No'. All the time that Paul was being frustrated and rebuffed, it was because God's plans were being worked out in his life—and that plan brought Christianity, for possibly the first time, out of the Near East and into Europe.

3 Convenient lies

Genesis 26:7–11

Many of the stories of Isaac have close parallels in the life of his father Abraham, and nowhere is it more true than in this one, where Isaac passes his wife off as his sister to ensure his own safety. There have already been two versions, in Genesis 12 and 20, and stories like this were obviously told and retold over time. This perhaps explains the anachronism in the narrative. Although Abimelek is called 'king of the Philistines' (v. 8), the Philistines did not settle in this area until some 600 years after the time of the patriarchs. So the story has been expressed in language and concepts familiar to a later reader. It is probable that the basic plot was familiar too—a man in a foreign land, claiming that his beautiful wife is his sister to keep himself from harm. This might explain the lack of detail given: if the plot is familiar, there is no need to fill in the details.

Our passage raises some interesting ethical questions. Many commentators have sought excuses for the lies told by Isaac and, earlier, by Abraham. Some have noted that Abraham premeditated the deceit (12:11–13), while Isaac seems to have reacted instinctively to save himself. Others point out that every case resulted in a blessing, so 'all's well that ends well'. But the fact remains that Isaac lied and deliberately put his wife in danger to save himself, for which he is criticised by most commentators. As it turned out, of course, Isaac's concerns for his safety were unfounded. Worries are often worse than the reality. As the French writer Michel de Montaigne once said, 'My life has been full of terrible misfortunes—most of which have never happened.' Unlike Sarah, Isaac's mother, Rebecca is kept safe and Abimelek acts as a perfect gentleman. However, given his family history, Isaac must have known that his actions were putting her in jeopardy.

In Hebrews 11, Isaac is held up as an example of a hero of faith, yet this passage in Genesis is a reminder that even the best of us are not perfect. As the old hymn put it, we are all 'prone to wander... prone to leave the God I love' (Robert Robinson, 1758). This passage also reminds us that lies have uncertain consequences. In Genesis 12, Sarah was taken into the harem of Pharaoh as a result of Abraham's lies. In chapter 20, she was saved from danger only by divine intervention. Here in Genesis 26, Rebecca is saved by Abimelek's chivalry. One lie—three consequences.

4 Does it work?

People today are getting more hard-headed. Influenced (though few realise it) by pragmatic philosophers like the 20th-century Frenchman Deleuze, people look at the world with less interest in whether something is true than whether it works. People may agree, objectively, with many of the arguments for Christianity, but they will be unmoved unless they see it in action. As the American writer Henry Adams said, 'What you do speaks so loudly, I cannot hear what you say.' Ephesians 4 suggests that Christianity ought to thrive in such a climate, because the Christian message ought to be visible in the lives of believers.

In Romans 12:2, Paul tells the believers not to 'conform any longer to the pattern of this world, but be transformed by the renewing of your mind'. It is that transformation that is being described in Ephesians 4. It is like removing an old garment, the old life, and putting on a new garment, new life in Christ (vv. 22–23). Our reading speaks of taking off lying and putting on truth; taking off anger and putting on peacefulness; taking off laziness and putting on hard work; taking off hurtful words and putting on words that build up. In short, it speaks about making choices in our lifestyle—choosing to speak truthfully rather than deceitfully.

People lie for a host of reasons. They lie out of fear, out of a need for acceptance, to get ahead, or perhaps out of habit, to make life easier. We see it all around us: 'The cheque is in the post'; 'It will only take five minutes'; 'Open wide, this won't hurt a bit.' Actually, to be fair, when the dentist said that to me, he was telling the truth. It did not hurt a bit—it hurt a lot. Ephesians says that lying has consequences not only for us but also for the relationships we form. We are all members of one body; we are all connected. We are all dependent on one another, and what hurts one hurts all.

But building up the body is not just a matter of putting off lying; it also means speaking the truth. I do not mean the hurtful truths that we avoid speaking ('That outfit makes you look fat'), but the many affirming truths that we neglect to mention to the people around us ('Your contribution to that debate was valuable'). These truths could be a huge encouragement, if they were shared and spoken.

5 Prosperity and prejudice

Genesis 26:12–17

Isaac prospered in Gerar: he planted crops and reaped a bumper harvest. This blessing is explained as divine. Even in good conditions, such a hundredfold return would be beyond the dreams of any farmer; coming as it did during a time of famine, it was doubly remarkable. Isaac's prosperity bred envy, and envy brought conflict. The land around Gerar (which today is called Tel Haror, in southern Israel) is fertile but very dry. In such a climate, control of wells and, therefore, access to water were vital for survival.

Abraham had been able to ensure access to watering holes through his military strength. Genesis 14:14 speaks of Abraham having 318 trained soldiers, as well as a network of military alliances. Isaac, however, does not seem to have been cut from the same cloth. The Philistines sensed weakness and sought to do to Isaac what they had not dared to do to Abraham—drive him away by denying him access to water. Despite the fact that, since his father's time, he had enjoyed a covenant alliance with the people of Gerar, Isaac responded to their hostility in a conciliatory manner: he moved a short distance away. Was he being meek, or was he being weak?

There are two perspectives to this story and two questions that we might like to consider. The first, from the perspective of Isaac, is: how do we react when we are unjustly treated? Do we insist on our rights, push back and stand up for ourselves, or do we turn the other cheek?

The other perspective is that of the Philistines. Their initial welcome of Isaac into their midst seems to have been generous and heartfelt—until he settled down and began to prosper. Then they became envious and hostile. Doesn't that sound familiar? It is an experience that would be echoed by many immigrant families throughout the ages. Many times the Bible draws on the experience of God's people as refugees to call for charitable and welcoming treatment for those who live among us. Exodus 22:21 reads, 'You shall not wrong or oppress a resident alien, for you were aliens in the land of Egypt' (NRSV). Perhaps we can learn and take warning from the attitude of the Philistines towards Isaac and not succumb to envy and prejudice.

6 Rebirth and renewal

Titus 3:1–8

The book of Titus covers many topics, from church government to the way Titus should conduct himself as a church leader and what he should teach. In chapter 3, after specific instructions to different groups in the church, Paul gives Titus a message for the whole church about how Christians should live. The new identity that is ours in Christ ought to change our attitudes. Our reading says that it should make us ready to do good works (v. 1) and devoted to good works (v. 8), out of gratitude for what has been done for us. Titus is urged to remember his old attitudes and old lifestyle, and to be encouraged by how far he has come. However, this journey does not give an excuse for arrogance; rather, it is a cause for gratitude: 'He saved us, not because of righteous things we had done, but because of his mercy' (v. 5).

Part of that transformation is to make us 'peaceable and considerate' (v. 2). For some (perhaps like Isaac), this comes fairly naturally. It is part of their basic temperament. For most of us, though, it is more of a struggle. For those of us who face this challenge, the good news is that changes in our character are not expected to come about by our own efforts. John 3:5 says that those entering the kingdom of God are born 'of water and the Spirit'. Titus 3 similarly speaks of the 'washing of rebirth and renewal by the Holy Spirit' (v. 5).

Using the language of baptism, Titus 3 speaks of 'rebirth' (*paliggenesia* in Greek). This is a rich theological word, used by the rabbis to describe the transformation of the world that the Messiah was to bring, but here it is about individual and personal transformation in the life of the believer. As Jesus teaches in John 3:3, becoming a Christian is nothing less than a complete restart, being born all over again.

This restart does not happen so that the same life can be lived over again, with the same mistakes and flaws. Titus 3:5 also speaks of spiritual 'renewal' (*anakainosis* in Greek), a word that has overtones of a change that is total and an improvement. We are used to seeing products described as 'new and improved'—and that is precisely what the Christian life is supposed to be.

Guidelines

The appeal of Isaac is not his strength; it is his vulnerability. He does not come across as the bravest or the strongest or the holiest. He lied; he backed down when challenged; he seemed never quite to fill his father's shoes.

God often uses weaknesses in people, as well as strengths. Perhaps, if Isaac had been more strong-willed, he would never have been content to remain in Gerar. Perhaps, if he had been braver, he would not ultimately have been reconciled with the Philistines (Genesis 26:31). As God says to Paul in 2 Corinthians 12:9, 'My grace is sufficient for you, for my power is made perfect in weakness.'

- How have you seen God at work despite the weakness and failings of people?
- Where in your life do you most need God's strength and help? Where are you weakest?
- How would you describe your spiritual life at the moment? Do you feel frustrated, like Paul in Asia? Do you feel that things are moving on with renewed purpose, as Paul did after he saw the vision of the Macedonian? Or do you feel slightly sidelined, like Isaac in Gerar?

Lord, I am not perfect. I am not strong. As the hymn says, 'I need thee, every hour.' I need thee to help me in my weakness, as I seek to live for thee. I need thee in my life, to give it purpose and direction. I need thee, oh, I need thee. Every hour, I need thee. Amen

29 April–5 May

1 Redigging the wells

Genesis 26:18

Today's reading is only one verse, but it is a key one in the life of Isaac and spiritually key for us as well. In our story so far, Isaac has been pictured as a fairly weak character whose every action seeks to avoid conflict. But there comes a point where he obviously feels that he needs to assert his position, so he reopens and renames the wells that were dug by his father. Both actions are important. Reopening the wells asserts his confidence and power, and naming them asserts his ownership. In one move, he answers any who have questioned his backbone and shows them that he is indeed his father's son.

Some commentators through the centuries have sought spiritual significance in this verse, as well. Images of water and wells, so essential to life, are used in the Bible many times as symbols of God's Spirit and refreshing presence—not least by Jesus himself, who said, 'If anyone thirsts, let him come to me and drink. Rivers of living water will brim and spill out of the depths of anyone who believes in me this way, just as the Scripture says' (John 7:37, THE MESSAGE).

Our verse today invites us to think, 'What spiritual wells have been dug in my life that, over the years, have become clogged up and need to be redug?' Many people start their Christian life with noble intentions that, over time, often become compromised and forgotten as other priorities take precedence, memory fades or enthusiasm wanes. Sometimes we need simply to remember, and redig the wells.

Perhaps there is a lesson here for churches, too. Every church has a spiritual legacy. There are deep wells of devotion, prayer, commitment and vision that lie behind the current generation in any church. The current congregation would do well to explore, draw from and, if necessary, redig these spiritual wells.

2 The cost of discipleship

Luke 9:57–62

Many church growth strategies seem to be built upon making Christianity as acceptable and unthreatening as possible, removing all the 'obstacles' that put people off. I wonder how such approaches deal with a passage like this one. When Jesus spoke about discipleship, he never minced words. He seemed to warn rather than welcome, and was content to turn people away rather than accept a half-hearted discipleship from them. Jesus made no easy promises about prosperity, security or happiness. He did not present a faith that was easy but, at the same time, bland and sterile. He emphasised cost, perseverance and sacrifice. The discipleship that Jesus offered could never be a hobby.

Our passage draws together three stories of would-be disciples, all of whom express their desire to follow Jesus but find that it is easier said than done. The first seems not to understand what being a disciple means. The second wants to fulfil his legal obligation to bury his father. The third wants first to say 'goodbye' to his family. The situations are different but the attitudes are the same. Each of them wants discipleship on their own convenient terms. Dietrich Bonhoeffer, the German pastor who opposed Hitler, wrote:

The trouble about this third would-be disciple is that at the very moment he expresses his willingness to follow, he ceases to want to follow at all. By making his offer on his own terms, he alters the whole position, for discipleship can tolerate no conditions which might come between Jesus and our obedience to him.
BONHOEFFER, THE COST OF DISCIPLESHIP

Jesus' words seem uncompromising, even harsh and cruel. Did Jesus really have a problem with someone burying their dead father? Did he object to people saying 'goodbye' to their families? No—but he did object to anything that got in the way of following him, because he knew that such easy, conditional discipleship at the outset would only lead to grief later on. We all hate hidden charges.

Jesus said, 'Follow me... and do not let anything else get in the way.' True discipleship is costly because it means putting Jesus before self. Is that unfair? Eugene Peterson, in his book *A Long Obedience in the Same Direction* (IVP, 2000), wrote, 'I have never yet heard a servant Christian complain about the oppressiveness of his servitude. I have never yet heard a servant Christian rail against the restrictions of her service. A servant Christian is the freest person on earth.'

3 Finding peace in a world of trouble

Genesis 26:19–23

So far, Isaac's actions in Genesis 26 have been an echo of his father's life. The author seems to be at pains to emphasise that Isaac was faithful to his father's legacy, and that the call of God to Abraham was continued by Isaac with little variation. Isaac continued Abraham's pattern of digging wells. However, he was not simply content to re-excavate the wells his father had dug; he also ordered his servants to dig new wells—and here, old problems and old conflicts resurfaced. The Philistines seem to have been content for him to reassert control over the wells dug by his father and traditionally held by his family, but there was immediate hostility once he began digging new wells and, by implication, moving into new areas.

The first two wells dug were called Esek (dispute) and Sitnah (opposition), because both caused arguments and were appropriated by Philistine herders. It is likely that this response was a simple power play. The Philistines did not need the wells or they would already have dug them themselves. Rather, they wanted Isaac to be forced away. They got their wish, as, in both cases, Isaac quickly retreated rather than fight. After a brief show of defiance in opening up his father's wells, it seems that Isaac's fundamentally cautious character reasserted itself.

Finally, Isaac came to a wide open area where he was able to dig a well with impunity. This well he named Rehoboth ('broad place').

The locations of Esek and Sitnah are unknown, since the Gerar valley is littered with ancient wells. Rehoboth has been identified with Wadu er-Ruhaibeh, a remote ancient town. It is easy to see why Isaac was not bothered there. It was in the middle of nowhere. After so much conflict, it is tempting to hear relief in Isaac's voice: 'Now the Lord has given us room and we will flourish in the land' (v. 22).

Then something strange happened. Having finally found a place where he was at peace and could flourish, Isaac seems to have left immediately for Beersheba. This journey is perhaps the most significant because, for the first time, Isaac is not being driven: he goes of his own free will. Beersheba was a place from Isaac's childhood memory. Abraham had settled there and, significantly, made a peace treaty with Abimelek there (Genesis 21:22–34). It was to Beersheba that Abraham and Isaac returned after the near-sacrifice of Isaac (22:19). It was a place that Isaac may have associated with peace and deliverance. Perhaps Isaac was on a spiritual journey as well as a physical one. Rehoboth had been a place of peace and plenty, but it was not a place of blessing. It was at Beersheba that Isaac would finally hear from God.

4 Teaching by example

2 Timothy 3:10–15

As we have seen over the past days, Isaac had many faults. He could be timid and was prone to being pushed around because he avoided conflict. But one characteristic cannot be criticised: Isaac kept on going. Over and over again, he dug wells, only to be moved on. His response? He started again and kept on digging.

Paul shared the same characteristic. Reading through the accounts of his missionary journeys in Acts, we cannot help but be amazed at his tenacity. Whatever was thrown at him, he kept coming back. When the Corinthian church accused him of being weak, he responded with an astonishing litany of struggles that he had endured for the sake of the gospel (2 Corinthians 11:23–27).

2 Timothy was written towards the end of Paul's ministry. He was in prison and ready to die (see 2:9; 4:6–8). He wrote to encourage Timothy to continue Paul's ministry, 'fanning into flame' the gifts that Timothy possessed (1:6), and also to give him warnings, for Paul had a notion that difficult times were ahead.

Paul urged Timothy to follow what he had learned from him. The NIV text of 2 Timothy 3:10 is a bit misleading: it says that Timothy 'knows' Paul's teaching. A better translation, perhaps, is that Timothy has 'followed' Paul's teaching. The Greek verb *parakoloutheo* means to 'follow after' or 'accompany'. It was the term used of a disciple following a rabbi, learning not just from his teaching but also by observing his character. In Timothy's case, he learned by sharing Paul's experiences and observing his purpose, faith, patience and so on.

We should not underestimate the teaching Timothy had received. He had heard Paul preach and had sat with him as he wrote 2 Corinthians (see 2 Corinthians 1:1). But our passage suggests that Paul's teaching was not divorced from his character. This was not always the case with religious leaders. Jesus said of the Pharisees, 'The teachers of the law and the Pharisees sit in Moses' seat. So you must obey them and do everything they tell you. But do not do what they do, for they do not practise what they preach' (Matthew 23:2–3). It goes without saying that this charge could not be levelled against Paul.

5 Called and blessed

Genesis 26:23–32

Beersheba was famous in Israel as one of the main cities and worship sites in southern Israel. 'From Dan [in the far north] to Beersheba [in the far south]' became a way of describing the whole country. This city was the site of a profound change in Isaac's fortunes. Politically, he was reconciled with Abimelek, and the conflict between the Philistines and Hebrews was brought to an end. Spiritually, he was blessed by God and that blessing was recognised by those around him.

What brought this change in fortunes? On a human level, we might think in terms of Isaac's growing prosperity and military strength, which made the Philistines think twice about antagonising him and forced Abimelek to seek a treaty with him. But our reading suggests a spiritual improvement in Isaac's fortunes, too. Until this point, Isaac's journeys have all been described using the Hebrew verb *halak*—the simple verb that means 'to walk' or 'go'. When he moves to Beersheba, however, the verb that is used is *alah*, 'to ascend'. Often in the Bible, encounters with God occur in high places, and the verb *alah* is used in a spiritual sense of 'going up' to meet God.

Certainly it is at Beersheba that God meets Isaac again and echoes the blessing he delivered in the opening verses of this chapter. Still the blessing is 'for the sake of' his father Abraham (one wonders what Isaac needs to do to get a blessing in his own right!) but it is made clear that 'the Lord was with' Isaac (v. 28). Perhaps there has been a spiritual change in him. Until now, his first action in any new area has been to dig a well and secure a water supply for his herds. In Beersheba, his first act is to build an altar and call on the name of the Lord; then he pitches his tent, and finally he digs a well (v. 25). Perhaps this denotes a change in policy; perhaps it denotes a change in heart. Certainly it establishes Isaac as the founder of Beersheba as a centre for worship and sacrifice.

Jesus said, 'Seek first the kingdom of God' (Matthew 6:33). Isaac at Beersheba sought first to worship God, and at Beersheba, for the first time in a long time, he knew peace and security.

6 The gift of God

John 4:3–11

Although we have been considering wells as places of worldly power and symbols of spiritual refreshment, they were also natural places for social gatherings. One such well was at Sychar, which was almost certainly at or near the site of Shechem, the ancient capital of Samaria. The well itself is one of the biblical sites that can be identified with certainty. It is a deep water source, now enclosed within an orthodox monastery, just off an ancient highway.

There is so much in this story that could be our focus today. Many writers have emphasised the social taboos that Jesus overcame in speaking to a Samaritan woman. There is also the contrast between the physical water that the woman was seeking and the living water that Jesus was offering. We could draw lessons from the transformation of the woman—how she turned from a sceptic into a witness, and effectively shared her testimony with her neighbours. Today, though, let us focus on one word in the story. It is in verse 10, and it is the word *dorea* in Greek, meaning 'gift'.

As we saw earlier in the week, Isaac was not easily put off. When he dug his wells, he often encountered opposition; but when he did, he just moved on and dug again. Each of those wells represented days of hard, unremitting toil in the heat of the sun. The Samaritan woman, too, worked hard for her water. The well at Sychar was 'deep' (v. 11) and it lay at least half a mile from the village. Even today, in much of the world, access to water is difficult. According to the charity Water Aid, many women and children spend up to six hours a day walking to fetch water. The load of water these women and children carry can be as much as 50 pounds in weight, roughly the same as an army pack.

It is small wonder, then, that the woman was attracted by the offer of water that would mean never being thirsty again! The water she collected was costly in time and labour. The water Jesus offered her was not the result of effort of her own. It was freely offered and freely given.

Guidelines

Sometimes the most profound prayers are the shortest. A while ago, during a Communion service, everyone in my church was encouraged to remember those who first inspired us or taught us the Christian faith. Some remembered ministers or Sunday school teachers or parents. Others remembered authors or hymn writers. Some remembered biblical characters. In the silence of Communion, these people were remembered and honoured, not by an eloquent prayer but simply by being named aloud. These were the people who dug spiritual wells in the lives of one congregation.

- Who are the people who dug spiritual 'wells' in your life? How would you describe their influence on you?
- Are those wells still producing clear water? Have any of them been filled in over the years? Do any of them need redigging?
- Jesus said, 'Whoever drinks the water I give him will never thirst. Indeed, the water I give him will become in him a spring of water welling up to eternal life' (John 4:14). What about the people you influence? How is the life in you a spring of water that brings refreshment and life to others? How, by your words and your lifestyle, are you seeking to be an example?

Heavenly Father, thank you for those who have shaped my life and my faith. Thank you for the Bible, which refreshes and teaches. Thank you that you promised refreshment for those who seek it, and light for those who need it. Above all, thank you for the promise in your word that 'with joy you will draw water from the wells of salvation' (Isaiah 12:3). Amen

FURTHER READING
Daryl T. Sanders, *The Man in the Middle: Isaac*, CreateSpace, 2010.

The BRF

Magazine

The Managing Editor writes...

'You have reached your destination.' These are perhaps some of the most comforting words we can hear from a recorded voice these days—certainly more welcome than 'Thank you for holding; your call is important to us' or 'Going up' (when you wanted to go down).

In this issue of the BRF Magazine, Jane Butcher describes how, for her and other members of the Barnabas Children's Ministry team, the sat-nav's congratulatory message is just the start of a challenging and fulfilling day's work, bringing the riches of the Bible to schools throughout the country. The team member's 'destination' may be the jumping-off point for a new generation of faith.

You're probably familiar, though, with the saying 'To travel hopefully is a better thing than to arrive' (Robert Louis Stevenson). It's great to reach a destination but, in the Christian walk, the journey itself is our day-to-day experience and continues for a lifetime.

BRF's online discipleship course, Foundations21, takes up this idea, offering four different 'pathways' from which to explore Christianity, and Chief Executive Richard Fisher writes about a new handbook, *Introducing Foundations21*, that explains how the course works. Perhaps you or someone you know needs a top-up of energy for the spiritual journey, a different way of seeing the landscape, or a place to begin their exploration. If so, Foundations21 could be the answer.

Of course, BRF continues to offer inspirational resources in the form of books (in print and, increasingly, for Kindle). As ever, there is a new Lent book for this year, *When You Pray* by Joanna Collicutt, which takes a reflective look at the Lord's Prayer in Luke's Gospel.

In addition, our 'Recommended reading' for this issue focuses on different aspects of love, and the need to travel hopefully in order to find and keep it. Paul's prayer for the Ephesians was that they would 'know the love of Christ that surpasses knowledge [and] be filled with all the fullness of God' (Ephesians 3:19, NRSV). Now that's a destination worth keeping in view!

Lisa Cherrett

Introducing Foundations21

Richard Fisher

What is Foundations21? How does it work? How can it benefit my church? These are the questions we set out to answer in a new handbook for church leaders, published last year.

We're very conscious that church leaders are under tremendous pressure. They face a host of demands on their time and energy, and they're often expected to be all things to all people. We believe that Foundations21 could be of great help to churches and their leaders as they face the challenge of how to help people to grow in their faith and their understanding of God's call on their lives as Christians, and how to live in response to that call—in other words, discipleship. We see Foundations21 as a tool that churches can use in a variety of different ways to suit the needs of different individuals and contexts.

We recognised that most busy church leaders probably don't have the luxury of time to register on Foundations21, browse through the wealth of resources that it offers and reflect on ways in which they might make use of it in their churches. We concluded that we needed to provide something that would communicate the essence of Foundations21 to ministers and lay leaders. So we came up with a short handbook (isn't it ironic that, although Foundations21 is entirely online, it still needs paper to point people to it!) that acts as a ready-reference resource. The aim was to explain the background and content of the Foundations21 'approach' and to outline ways in which it might be used within the life of the church.

Introducing Foundations21 was published in February 2012. It outlines our vision for lifelong Christian learning to be accessible to everyone; for discipleship not to be something that we 'do' but something that becomes a way of life; to move away from a traditional 'one-size-fits-all' approach and offer something more flexible.

It unpacks our innovative 'four pathways' approach, enabling everyone to discover their preferred learning style and how each of these styles is linked to a Gospel. Are you a Matthew, Mark, Luke or John-type learner? (Why not go to www.foundations21.net and find out?)

Having outlined the Foundations21 approach, what it provides and how it all works, the handbook goes on to consider in more detail how the resource could be used in particular contexts in the life of the local church—for example, small groups, nurturing new Christians, one-to-one mentoring, preaching. I wonder if any of the following scenarios exist within your own congregation.

New Christians

Sarah and Max have just completed a Christian basics course. Jane has just been confirmed. They've been encouraged to start Foundations21, each accompanied by a more experienced member of the congregation to support and encourage them. Both they and the 'older, wiser' Christians with whom they've been paired in these 'buddy' relationships are enjoying taking these next steps together—and, perhaps to their surprise, the mature Christians are finding that they are learning just as much themselves.

Hungry Christians

John has recently retired and now finally has more time to explore his Christian faith in the way that he's always wanted to. Emma has been a Christian for a while, regularly attending her local church. Recently she's felt a real desire to know more and to go deeper with God. The usual diet of Sunday sermon and midweek group doesn't provide enough for John or Emma. They're hungry to go further and deeper, but they're not ready to do a formal course of study or training.

Disconnected Christians

Peter travels a great deal as part of his job; Sue has a long commute to work; Andrew works shifts that change frequently; Anita has three small children and is constantly juggling priorities and demands; James cares for elderly parents, so is often away at the weekend; Katherine is in the armed forces and never seems to be in one place for very long. For all these reasons, they, and many others like them, find it difficult to participate actively in the small group life of their church; they may even find it difficult to attend Sunday services on a regular basis.

Foundations21 could be one way to help all of these individuals.

Introducing Foundations21 also includes comments and testimonies from church leaders and individual users who have found Foundations21 to be of value. For example, one minister told us:

I used Foundations 21 to prepare an adult baptism candidate, as she was fairly new to faith. We went through the joining process together and dis-

cussed where she might begin and what rooms she might visit first. We were then able to catch up on what had been useful and what questions she had, the next time we met. I particularly valued using Foundations21 as it gave my candidate the opportunity to set her own agenda for exploring her faith while enabling me to keep pace with her because I had access to the same material. It also meant that she could keep exploring and journeying in her faith with Foundations21 after the baptism.

One of the keys to enabling churches to make the most of what Foundations21 has to offer is to find a Foundations21 'champion'. Consider all the initiatives and programmes that churches run effectively and successfully; it's unlikely that they do so without one or more individuals who have taken responsibility for them, who champion them. They don't happen by themselves! We at BRF are keen to develop and support a network of Foundations21 champions, who in turn can help and encourage individuals and groups in their own church communities as we all explore, learn and grow on our discipleship journey.

Foundations21 user Paula said:

I have now been a member of Foundations21 since November 2006. Initially I was looking for a well-balanced follow-on course from Alpha. Foundations21 certainly fits the bill! However, for me it has been much more than just a course. Yes, it does provide information, but also reflection and inspiration. It has turned out to be a companion on my Christian journey, constantly challenging my opinions and my lifestyle. Every time I return there is more to discover or reconsider. Foundations21 is a fantastic resource and one I hope to use for many years to come.

The Bishop of Oxford has written:

Foundations21 is an inspired and inspiring gift to the churches. This programme is deep and wide. It's flexible and user-friendly. Above all, it gives Christians and enquirers something to bite on, engage with and learn from.'

It's our prayer at BRF that God would use Foundations21 to transform lives and to help people embrace the lifelong challenge of what it means to follow Jesus today.

Do the leaders in your church know about Foundations21? If not, please do encourage them to take a look! Could you be a Foundations21 champion in your church? If so, we'd love to hear from you!

Introducing Foundations21 is available online in PDF form via the website www.foundations21.net (or directly from www.brf.org.uk/pdfs/Introducing_Foundations21.pdf), making it accessible to anyone who is interested, wherever they are in the world.

Barnabas RE Days

Jane Butcher

'You have reached your destination.' It's 8.00 on Wednesday morning and your trusty satnav companion has navigated you safely to the school car park. Next step: unload the car, make your way to Reception in the hope that a warm welcome (and a cup of coffee) will greet you, and thus the day unfolds.

Such is the start of many an RE Day. From this point on, what happens can vary from school to school. We generally find ourselves located in the school hall, which provides enough space for the interactive workshops.

Our team members have a host of different gifts and abilities and will deliver the workshops using their particular skill set, whether that be drama, storytelling, mime, music or dance. Whatever the style or theme, the focus remains the same—that, as adults and children, we journey together, exploring aspects of the Christian faith in a fun, inter-active and reflective way.

Generally we will do that through several 45-minute sessions with a group of up to 35 children in each, which could offer the opportunity to work with 280 children and their staff during the day.

By the end of the afternoon, it is not uncommon to feel exhausted, yet motivated and often humbled by a child's comment or observation, which has reminded us that we can learn so much from them. We are often refreshed by the children's openness and honesty. So the day ends: repack the boxes, load the car, turn on the satnav and 'navigate to home'.

One thing that is absolutely clear is that we could not do these days without the freelance team. We are blessed to have such a gifted team who enable us to meet the requests of schools across the UK. The following reflections are from two members of that team. First, we hear from Ken Wylie, who starting leading RE Days about four years ago:

'RE days are full of buzz. I have to give out more than I expect to receive back in terms of energy but I normally come away from a day in a school with a fresh insight into the theme, and smiling over some comment or incident from the day. It is sometimes like being a stand-up comic, needing to deal with anything that might present itself, such as the quickfire comments that children can shoot out, whether they're 4 or 11 years old.

'It is very gratifying to see the excitement of children in the sessions, and their total involvement in a particular story or activity. I feel that, by now, I should not be surprised by their responses as, so often, they have incredibly perceptive views. The downside is that we are only in a school for one day, so I always hope that teachers are able to benefit from hearing their charges expressing themselves in new ways or offering a window into their lives outside school. A real reward comes when we hear about a normally disruptive pupil who has been able to connect with and fully participate in the creative approach that Barnabas in Schools offers.

'In one Year 4 class, looking at the theme "Whose world?", we had explored what Genesis 1 has to say about creation and had worked out that God's perfect world is no longer perfect and it's up to us to do something about it. Coming into the last couple of minutes of my time with them, one girl gave this comment: "It's good that the world isn't perfect, otherwise we would have nothing to dream for."

'No two days are the same, so there is never room for complacency. Of course, the "success" of any day is heavily influenced by the prayers of BRF partners and supporters. Thank you, and please keep praying.'

The following reflection comes from new team member Sean Arberry, who has recently joined us in Cornwall.

'Speaking from my experience over my first few workshops, sometimes children can imagine RE to be dull: obviously, it's not football or *The X-Factor*! But it feels great when you engage them at the first assembly in the morning with something fun, like an interactive telling of "The Rock", and then, through the workshops, see them find out how exciting it all is. One fabulous highlight for me came during a "Who Comes First?" session, when the children played the disciples being called by Jesus for the first time, and posed for a team photo, having all just become winners. This team of disciples was made up from a complete mixture of talents and foibles, yet it changed the world. It was something that the children could easily identify with.'

Your prayers are so important to us—particularly for safe travel. So, to return to Ken's words, 'Thank you, and please keep praying.'

For more information on Barnabas RE Days, please visit: www.barnabasinschools.org.uk.

Recommended reading

The theme of love runs deep through our book selection for the start of this new year. Naomi Starkey explores the search for love that envelops all our lives at one time or another, asking, 'Do we really understand what we are searching for?' and Veronica Zundel explores the love between parents and their children and how the outworking of that love reveals God's love for us as his children. Then, from the pages of *Woman Alive* magazine, a new author to BRF tells her story of searching for love through the increasingly popular internet dating sites.

The Recovery of Love
Walking the way to wholeness
Naomi Starkey

The world's hunger for love can be met only in God's never-ending embrace, but, before that hunger can be understood, one question must be pondered and answered: what does the world really want? *The Recovery of Love* begins in an unnamed city, which evokes the stress and demands endemic to life in today's busy, predominantly urban culture. It embodies emptiness and despair. It ends in the same city, but this city now reverberates with a little of the imagery of the city of God, the new Jerusalem. In between, we are taken to explore a curious yet safe place, a mysterious house of many rooms where questions can be asked, experiences shared and the search for healing begun.

At the heart of the story is the meaning of love—on the one hand, our hunger for it and our often weary search to find and secure it, and, on the other hand, God's breathtaking love for us.

Ref: 978 1 84101 892 8, paperback, 160 pages, £6.99
Kindle edition: 978 0 85746 196 4, £6.99

Everything I Know about God, I've Learned from Being a Parent
Veronica Zundel

The Bible tells us that God is 'the Father, from whom every family in heaven and on earth takes its name' (Ephesians 3:15). If earthly families gain their nature from God's parenthood, what might our experience of family tell us about the nature of God? That is the question on which this book focuses.

Veronica Zundel roots her reflections in her journey into and through parenthood, a hard journey that led through infertility, late motherhood and then learning to parent a child with special needs. What she learned along the way—about love and sacrifice, faithfulness and forgiveness—had a profound impact on her understanding of what God feels about us, his most beloved children.

Ref: 978 1 84101 416 6, paperback, 144 pages, £6.99
Kindle edition: 978 0 85746 198 8

Would Like to Meet
The real-life diary of a 30-something Christian woman looking for love
Hopefulgirl

Shares the ups and downs of a 30-something Christian woman, looking for love after the ending of an eight-year relationship (just as she and her partner were seriously planning a future together). She ventures into the world of Christian dating via the internet, and tries to find 'The One' in a context where single women outnumber single men by a massive margin. She debates questions such as 'How easily can "liking" turn into "love"?' 'What about dating/marrying non-Christians?', 'What to do when the biological clock is ticking and nobody seems to "click" with you?' Along the way, she meets and wonders about TinyMan, CrewCutMan, TeacherMan, BeardyMan, TechniMan and HaughtyMan.

Ref: 978 0 85746 152 0, paperback, 160 pages, £6.99
Kindle edition: 978 0 85746 200 8

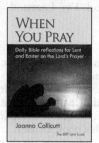

WHEN YOU PRAY

Daily Bible reflections for Lent and Easter on the Lord's Prayer

Joanna Collicutt

The BRF Lent book

The BRF Lent Book

BRF's Lent book for 2013, *When You Pray*, shows how growing as a Christian is rooted in the prayer Jesus gave us. As we pray the Lord's Prayer, we not only express our relationship with God, we absorb gospel values and are motivated to live them out. In her Introduction, author Joanna Collicutt writes:

The Lord's Prayer contains all that Christians really need to know; it is the very essence of the gospel. This understanding of the Lord's Prayer is not at all new. It was the practice of the early church to prepare candidates for baptism during Lent by teaching them the Lord's Prayer and using it as the basis for instruction in the faith, sometimes supported by the creeds… It was wise of those very early Christians to use a prayer rather than a set of statements to prepare people for a life of faith, for faith is not our beliefs about God; it is, rather, the relationship of trust with God that we live out… Praying the Lord's Prayer is an expression of and vehicle for our relationship with God…

In praying the Lord's Prayer, human beings take on the character of Christ. We don't just act in obedience to Christ or in conformity with Christ… In some very deep sense, which I hope to explore in this series of biblical reflections, we are incorporated into Christ and are 'in union' with Christ. Lent is, after all, the period in which Christians have traditionally sought to identify more deeply with Christ.

As Paul discovered, this is a transforming work of the Spirit, but it is also a work that is wrought through the medium of words. The words are very important, and the most important of them is *Abba*, for through the work of Christ human beings are offered the possibility of an intimate parental relationship with the divine. Here, at the outset, we find a trinitarian framework: we pray in union with Christ through the power of the Spirit, and our prayer is directed to the Father…

My prayer for those who read this book is that you will have a sense of the great privilege that has been granted to us of holding a precious gem in our hands, of being able to delight in its radiance, play with its many facets, plumb its depths, gain a sense of peace and security from its touch, and in so doing deepen our awareness of our union with Christ.

To order a copy of this book, please turn to the order form on page 153 or visit www.brfonline.org.uk. This book is also available for Kindle.

SUPPORTING BRF'S MINISTRY

As a Christian charity, BRF is involved in seven distinct yet complementary areas.

- **BRF** (www.brf.org.uk) resources adults for their spiritual journey through Bible reading notes, books and Quiet Days. BRF also provides the infrastructure that supports our other specialist ministries.
- **Foundations21** (www.foundations21.net) provides flexible and innovative ways for individuals and groups to explore their Christian faith and discipleship through a multimedia internet-based resource
- **Messy Church** (www.messychurch.org.uk), led by Lucy Moore, enables churches all over the UK (and increasingly abroad) to reach children and adults beyond the fringes of the church.
- **Barnabas in Churches** (www.barnabasinchurches.org.uk) helps churches to support, resource and develop their children's ministry with the under-11s more effectively .
- **Barnabas in Schools** (www.barnabasinschools.org.uk) enables primary school children and teachers to explore Christianity creatively and bring the Bible alive within RE and Collective Worship.
- **Faith in Homes** (www.faithinhomes.org.uk) supports families to explore and live out the Christian faith at home.
- **Who Let The Dads Out** (www.wholetthedadsout.org) inspires churches to engage with dads and their pre-school children.

At the heart of BRF's ministry is a desire to equip adults and children for Christian living—helping them to read and understand the Bible, explore prayer and grow as disciples of Jesus. We need your help to make an impact on the local church, local schools and the wider community.

- You could support BRF's ministry with a donation or standing order (using the response form overleaf).
- You could consider making a bequest to BRF in your will.
- You could encourage your church to support BRF as part of your church's giving to home mission—perhaps focusing on a specific area of our ministry, or a particular member of our Barnabas team.
- Most important of all, you could support BRF with your prayers.

If you would like to discuss how a specific gift or bequest could be used in the development of our ministry, please phone 01865 319700 or email enquiries@brf.org.uk.

Whatever you can do or give, we thank you for your support.

BRF MINISTRY APPEAL RESPONSE FORM

Name _____

Address _____

_____ Postcode _____

Telephone _____ Email _____

Gift Aid Declaration

❏ I am a UK taxpayer. I want BRF to treat as Gift Aid Donations all donations I make from 6 April 2000 until I notify you otherwise.

Signature _____ Date _____

❏ I would like to support BRF's ministry with a regular donation by standing order

Standing Order – Banker's Order

To the Manager, Name of Bank/Building Society

Address _____

_____ Postcode _____

Sort Code _____ Account Name _____

Account No _____

Please pay Royal Bank of Scotland plc, Drummonds, 49 Charing Cross,
London SW1A 2DX (Sort Code 16-00-38), for the account of BRF A/C No. 00774151

The sum of _____ pounds on ___/___/___ (insert date) and thereafter the same amount on the same day each month / same day annually (delete as applic.) until further notice.

Signature _____ Date _____

Single donation

❏ I enclose my cheque/credit card/Switch card details for a donation of
£5 £10 £25 £50 £100 £250 (other) £ _____ to support BRF's ministry

Card no.																

Expires				Security code				Issue no.			

Signature _____ Date _____

Please use my donation for ❏ BRF ❏ Foundations21 ❏ Messy Church
❏ Barnabas for Children ❏ Faith in Homes

❏ Please send me information about making a bequest to BRF in my will.

Please detach and send this completed form to: Richard Fisher, BRF,
15 The Chambers, Vineyard, Abingdon OX14 3FE. BRF is a Registered Charity (No.233280)

Please ensure that you complete and send off both sides of this order form.

Please send me the following book(s):

		Quantity	Price	Total
089 9	When You Pray (*J. Collicutt*)	_____	£7.99	_____
892 8	The Recovery of Love (*N. Starkey*)	_____	£6.99	_____
152 0	Would Like to Meet (*HopefulGirl*)	_____	£6.99	_____
416 6	Everything I Know about God… (*V. Zundel*)	_____	£6.99	_____
046 2	Paul as Pastor (*P. Whitworth*)	_____	£8.99	_____
798 3	The Way of the Desert (*A. Watson*)	_____	£7.99	_____
704 4	Jesus Christ—the Alpha & the Omega (*N.G. Wright*)	_____	£7.99	_____
680 1	Giving It Up (*M. Dawn*)	_____	£7.99	_____
814 0	Messy Cooks (*J. Butcher*)	_____	£5.99	_____
049 3	Family Fun for Easter (*J. Butcher*)	_____	£4.99	_____
061 5	Family Fun for Summer (*J. Butcher*)	_____	£4.99	_____

Total cost of books £ _____

Donation £ _____

Postage and packing £ _____

TOTAL £ _____

POSTAGE AND PACKING CHARGES				
order value	UK	Europe	Surface	Air Mail
£7.00 & under	£1.25	£3.00	£3.50	£5.50
£7.01–£30.00	£2.25	£5.50	£6.50	£10.00
Over £30.00	free	prices on request		

For more information about new books and special offers, visit www.brfonline.org.uk.

See over for payment details.

All prices are correct at time of going to press, are subject to the prevailing rate of VAT and may be subject to change without prior warning.

PAYMENT DETAILS

WAYS TO ORDER BRF RESOURCES

Christian bookshops: All good Christian bookshops stock BRF publications. For your nearest stockist, please contact BRF.

Telephone: The BRF office is open between 09.15 and 17.30.
To place your order, phone 01865 319700; fax 01865 319701.

Web: Visit www.brfonline.org.uk

By post: Please complete the payment details below and send with appropriate payment and completed order form to:

BRF, 15 The Chambers, Vineyard, Abingdon OX14 3FE

Name _____

Address _____

_____ Postcode _____

Telephone _____

Email _____

Total enclosed £ _____ (cheques should be made payable to 'BRF')

Please charge my Visa ❑ Mastercard ❑ Switch card ❑ with £ _____

Card no: ⬜⬜⬜⬜⬜⬜⬜⬜⬜⬜⬜⬜⬜⬜⬜⬜⬜⬜⬜⬜

Expires ⬜⬜⬜⬜ Security code ⬜⬜⬜

Issue no (Switch only) ⬜⬜

Signature (essential if paying by credit/Switch) _____

❑ Please do not send me further information about BRF publications.

BRF is a Registered Charity

GUIDELINES SUBSCRIPTIONS

Please note our subscription rates 2013–2014. From the May 2013 issue, the new subscription rates will be:

Individual subscriptions covering 3 issues for under 5 copies, payable in advance (including postage and packing):

	UK	SURFACE	AIRMAIL
GUIDELINES each set of 3 p.a.	£15.00	£21.60	£24.00
GUIDELINES 3-year sub i.e. 9 issues	£37.80	N/A	N/A

Group subscriptions covering 3 issues for 5 copies or more, sent to ONE UK address (post free).

GUIDELINES	£12.00	each set of 3 p.a.

Overseas group subscription rates available on request.
Contact enquiries@brf.org.uk.

Please note that the annual billing period for Group Subscriptions runs from 1 May to 30 April.

Copies of the notes may also be obtained from Christian bookshops:

GUIDELINES	£4.00 each copy

Visit www.biblereadingnotes.org.uk for information about our other Bible reading notes and Apple apps for iPhone and iPod touch.

❏ I would like to take out a subscription myself:

Your name _____

Your address _____

_____ Postcode _____

Tel _____ Email _____

Please send *Guidelines* beginning with the May 2013 / September 2013 / January 2014 issue: (delete as applicable)

(please tick box)	UK	SURFACE	AIR MAIL
GUIDELINES	❏ £15.00	❏ £21.60	❏ £24.00
GUIDELINES 3-year sub	❏ £37.80		
GUIDELINES pdf download	❏ £12.00 (UK and overseas)		

Please complete the payment details below and send with appropriate payment to: **BRF, 15 The Chambers, Vineyard, Abingdon OX14 3FE**

Total enclosed £ _____ (cheques should be made payable to 'BRF')

Please charge my Visa ❏ Mastercard ❏ Switch card ❏ with £

Card no: | | | | | | | | | | | | | | | | | | |

Expires | | | | | Security code | | | |

Issue no (Switch only) | | | | |

Signature (essential if paying by card) _____

To set up a direct debit, please also complete the form on page 159 and send it to BRF with this form.

BRF is a Registered Charity

GUIDELINES GIFT SUBSCRIPTIONS

❏ I would like to give a gift subscription (please provide both names and addresses:

Your name _____

Your address _____

_____ Postcode _____

Tel _____ Email _____

Gift subscription name _____

Gift subscription address _____

_____ Postcode _____

Gift message (20 words max. or include your own gift card for the recipient)

_____

_____

Please send *Guidelines* beginning with the May 2013 / September 2013 / January 2014 issue: (delete as applicable)

(please tick box)	UK	SURFACE	AIR MAIL
GUIDELINES	❏ £15.00	❏ £21.60	❏ £24.00
GUIDELINES 3-year sub	❏ £37.80		
GUIDELINES pdf download	❏ £12.00 (UK and overseas)		

Please complete the payment details below and send with appropriate payment to: **BRF, 15 The Chambers, Vineyard, Abingdon OX14 3FE**

Total enclosed £ _____ (cheques should be made payable to 'BRF')

Please charge my Visa ❏ Mastercard ❏ Switch card ❏ with £

Card no: [ ][ ][ ][ ][ ][ ][ ][ ][ ][ ][ ][ ][ ][ ][ ][ ][ ][ ]

Expires [ ][ ][ ][ ] Security code [ ][ ][ ]

Issue no (Switch only) [ ][ ][ ]

Signature (essential if paying by card) _____

To set up a direct debit, please also complete the form on page 159 and send it to BRF with this form.

Now you can pay for your annual subscription to BRF notes using Direct Debit. You need only give your bank details once, and the payment is made automatically every year until you cancel it. If you would like to pay by Direct Debit, please use the form opposite, entering your BRF account number under 'Reference'.

You are fully covered by the Direct Debit Guarantee:

The Direct Debit Guarantee

- This Guarantee is offered by all banks and building societies that accept instructions to pay Direct Debits.
- If there are any changes to the amount, date or frequency of your Direct Debit, The Bible Reading Fellowship will notify you 10 working days in advance of your account being debited or as otherwise agreed. If you request The Bible Reading Fellowship to collect a payment, confirmation of the amount and date will be given to you at the time of the request.
- If an error is made in the payment of your Direct Debit, by The Bible Reading Fellowship or your bank or building society, you are entitled to a full and immediate refund of the amount paid from your bank or building society.
  - – If you receive a refund you are not entitled to, you must pay it back when The Bible Reading Fellowship asks you to.
- You can cancel a Direct Debit at any time by simply contacting your bank or building society. Written confirmation may be required. Please also notify us.

The Bible Reading Fellowship

Instruction to your bank or building society to pay by Direct Debit

Please fill in the whole form using a ballpoint pen and send to The Bible Reading Fellowship, 15 The Chambers, Vineyard, Abingdon OX14 3FE.

Service User Number: | 5 | 5 | 8 | 2 | 2 | 9 |

Name and full postal address of your bank or building society

To: The Manager	Bank/Building Society
Address	
	Postcode

Name(s) of account holder(s)

Branch sort code	Bank/Building Society account number

Reference

Instruction to your Bank/Building Society

Please pay The Bible Reading Fellowship Direct Debits from the account detailed in this instruction, subject to the safeguards assured by the Direct Debit Guarantee.
I understand that this instruction may remain with The Bible Reading Fellowship and, if so, details will be passed electronically to my bank/building society.

Signature(s)	
Date	

Banks and Building Societies may not accept Direct Debit instructions for some types of account.

This page is intentionally left blank.